# JOHN CROW SPEAKS

### Earth Teachings
### of the Jamaican Elders

# JOHN CROW SPEAKS

## Earth Teachings
## of the Jamaican Elders

**told by**

# Chet Alexander

MONKFISH BOOK PUBLISHING COMPANY
RHINEBECK, NEW YORK

Contact the publisher for information:
Monkfish Book Publishing Company
27 Lamoree Rd.
Rhinebeck, N.Y. 12572

Monkfish Memoirs, Volume 4

Printed in the United States of America
Book design by Mary Giddens
Cover design by Georgia Dent

Library of Congress Cataloging-in-Publication Data

Alexander, Chet, 1955-
    John Crow speaks : teachings of the Jamaican elders / Chet
Alexander.
        p. cm.
    ISBN 0-9749359-4-8
    1. Spiritual life. 2. Maroons--Jamaica--Religion--Miscellanea. I.
Title.
    BL624.A427 2005
    299'.93--dc22

                                    2005015330

Bulk purchase discounts for educational or promotional purposes are
available.

First edition

First impression

10 9 8 7 6 5 4 3 2 1

Monkfish Book Publishing Company
27 Lamoree Road
Rhinebeck, New York 12572
www.monkfishpublishing.com

# Contents

# Meeting the Earth Teacher

IN JAMAICA, when I was young, I often stayed at my grandfather's dairy farm at Montego Bay in the summer to help with the cows and the pimento harvest. Grandfather was descended from Native Americans, Africans, and Europeans. He was one of the people and they called him Maas Jim or Uncle Jim. He was not my grandfather by blood but because he married my grandmother after her husband died.

Grandfather's cows were raised organically, and their milk was frothy and rich compared to what most people drink and think is real milk. That morning, sitting on turned-over buckets, my cousins and I milked the cows, while we took turns squirting some of the warm, creamy liquid into each others' mouth.

As usual, after we drove the milk to the dairy by six o'clock, we went for a swim at Rosehall beach, where there were no hotels or tourists. Then we headed back to the farm to help with the pimento harvest until supper time.

The pimento harvest on my grandfather's land was a way for many local people to make extra cash. Bredda Man came to work on the harvest, and that is how I first met him.

Bredda Man was a country man, in the Jamaican sense this means he lived in an "Ital" way—an honest, natural way, close to the land, eating fresh foods. He was middle-aged. He didn't drive a car or work for other people doing jobs he didn't enjoy. He was an artist and made a living by selling his carvings in an art gallery in Kingston. He also worked for my grandfather at the farm and was one of my grandfather's most long-term and respected employees.

Bredda Man's appearance was striking. His features were definitely mixed blood, with the slanted eyes and high cheek-bones of the Native American, and the dark skin and strong features of the African. He didn't have a beard, and his black hair was long and straight.

He spoke with great fondness of his people, many of whom were mixed blood from Arawak and Maroon ancestors. He told me his mother was Arawak and his father was Maroon and that they lived in Acumpung, a large Maroon community in the Cockpit country.

Maroons were still practicing the "old ways" when I was a child. They were the only people on the island who weren't Christian, and they were considered a world apart from the other islanders. They lived in communities in the wildest parts of the country, completely separate from the rest of Jamaican colored people, since the 1600s when they had established their freedom as runaway slaves. They were feared and respected as warriors, and also sought after as healers for their medicinal knowledge. They spoke their own language and held their own ceremonies and rituals, independent of the rest of the cultural developments on the island.

It was in the way he walked that Bredda Man was taken for a Maroon. If you have ever met a Maroon you will understand what I speak about. Maroons walk different. There is a certain uprightness in their walk, a belonging to nature that is unafraid and strong. The bush was part of their life and their blood.

Those I met were fearless. All the Maroons I have met were also trustworthy people. I think their trustworthiness comes from that fearless quality.

There was one thing about Bredda Man that I will never forget. He always looked clean, and he smelled clean, even when he was in sweaty old work clothes. His cleanness came from the inside and radiated out of every pore of his skin.

He used herbal teas, oils, and remedies made from fresh, homegrown and wildcrafted herbs. I remember watching him rub his skin once with oil. He was very focused and serious, "It's medicine I'm rubbing in. Yes, maan … this rubbing is good medicine!"

Bredda Man was a healer. Although he never took money or boasted about his healing work, mysterious strangers found their way to his doorstep, and well-known doctors and healers came from far away to see him.

Bredda Man said there were many Maroon customs and traditions, which most Jamaican people did not know about, that had come from secret meetings in the bush of the wise elders among the early Arawaks, African medicine people, European Kabbalists and Masons.

For the most part Jamaicans today have forgotten the bush and any sacred role she plays. She is thought of mostly as a common Jamaican stereotype—a poor unappreciated mother with many children to feed.

After the abolition of slavery was read out in Spanish Town by one of my Jewish ancestors, many colored people saw Christianity as a way for them to be accepted into mainstream culture and the powerful stratas of Jamaican society. But the wise African elders saw Christianity as a way to carry the deities of the African pantheon into future generations. Christian saints were given the place of the "Loas," or gods and goddesses of Obeah (Voudou): John the Baptist became the countenance of Legba, the opener of gates and master of the crossroads; Moses, whose totem and standard honored the serpent and who healed and cursed using the serpent, became the invocation of Damballah the snake God of the stars; and the blessed Virgin Mary evoked Erzulie, the Heavenly Mother Goddess.

Those who didn't become Christian were regarded as outsiders and were looked upon with suspicion. But this also served the purpose of the Obeah and African elders to drive nosey, inquisitive busybodies away and to promote an aura of mystery that kept people open to the need for the traditional spiritual rituals.

Obeah and African cultures, however, have been watered down over the years as they have blended with Christianity. Outside of "Maroon town," Jamaica has become a melting pot for race, culture and spirituality. There is a saying in the islands, even today, the population is "ninety-percent Christian and one-hundred-percent Obeah."

Bredda Man was neither a Christian, nor a Maroon, and he also set himself apart from many of the Rastas on the island because he never drank alcohol or smoked *ganjah* (marijuana). In this way, Bredda Man chose to rely on himself for his path in life and to chart his own destiny.

\*   \*   \*

We were out in the bush, cutting pimento with long poles that had short, scissor-like cutting shears on the ends. As we pulled with a long rope, the shears clipped off the branches laden with the green and purple-black fruit. The pickers went from tree to tree with the shears, while others gathered the branches and brought them to the place where the shellers sat and stripped the branches clean of the berries.

The berries were piled into big crocus (sack cloth) bags, which were taken to the drying pens where they were spread out in large wooden bushel boxes and left until they got hard and black. The peppery oil rubbed into our clothes and hands, and after a while it helped to keep the mosquitoes away. We also collected dried cow dung patties for burning. As they slowly burned, we placed the green pimento leaves on top to make a pungent smoke. This smelled good, and it kept us free of ticks.

When we brought the pimento to the drying pens, we weighed our bags, and at the end of the day's harvest we collected our notes for payment. I always put my bags in with Bredda Man's, so he could get paid more. It was my own work, and I could do whatever I wanted with my pickings.

I didn't realize it at the time, but the elders, including my grandfather, regarded my generosity as a sign that I was a good-hearted person. Back then, one was respected for taking care of one's elders in kind, simple ways.

As we watched the pickers and shellers unloading the bags from the mules into the wooden boxes, Bredda Man lit one of his shags. These were cigarettes that he rolled from the tobacco he grew in his garden. They were really strong because the pure, raw tobacco leaves were not bleached or cut.

On special occasions, Bredda Man smoked a pipe, given to him by a Native American elder, which smelled mostly like a bush fire, though every now and again a sweet scent wafted from it through the air. This pipe was used only with the herbal mixtures Bredda Man gathered and dried himself. Except, Bredda Man told me, he had a friend who sent him mistletoe from out in St. Elizabeth that he sometimes used with the tobacco. Another herb I knew of, susumba leaves, was also sometimes mixed with the tobacco.

Bredda Man asked me to walk with him toward a small clearing. Some of the other men watched closely as we walked together, gesturing respectfully to Bredda Man and smiling kindly at me. I was excited. I knew that some young boys were chosen to be taught by the elders. Such boys were considered attentive and good hearted, and everyone respected them. Although I didn't really have a concern then for being respected, I felt drawn to learn from Bredda Man.

"Come, we will build a fire and boil some water," Bredda Man said, and he motioned for me to follow him.

I watched as he peeled dry wiss (vine) and arranged coconut husk fibers into a ball. Then he gathered some twigs and dry wood from the bush. I helped, knowing that I was expected to pay close attention to every detail.

When we had gathered enough wood and twigs together, he produced a small piece of flint and an iron striker.

As I watched Bredda Man building the fire, I felt honored to be asked to share and help. His movements and body language showed the attitude and deep reverence he held for the elements in nature. For me to learn his movements, I, too, would have to hold this reverence in my heart.

In Jamaican tradition learning by imitation—without asking questions—was still practiced because it ensured that a quality of heart was passed on in the ways people did things. Unless a person is attentive to the inner silence, the mind cannot retain what the body sees and feels. If we don't rely on asking questions, our impatience and passions are sacrificed to the silence. As compensation, the sharp attention necessary to recognize emotional signatures in body language is developed. It is easier to learn something, once the emotional signature in a movement is recognized.

With this method of learning people also gave up the

assumption that they could demand knowledge from another person. It was important to learn that feeding and empowering the silence was the way to encourage elders to help. If a person was good hearted and focused in silence, if he worked courageously and cheerfully, he would gain the favor and respect of the elders.

In the simple practice of imitation, I realized that, even more so than the teacher, the atmosphere and responsibility for learning is the work of the student.

Bredda Man held the flint and striker so that the sparks would fly toward the small ball of wiss and coconut fibers. He pulled out some cotton squares and put these against the fibers and wiss. When a few sparks caught in the blackened cotton fibers, he blew on the wiss and the smoldering ball of dried fibers until it burst into flame. Then he started to move the twigs and kindling into the small bundle. He blew again, and soon the entire kindling pile was on fire.

I had never seen a fire started without matches before. It was a truly beautiful sight to behold. The whole event felt magical to me.

Then Bredda Man sent me to get the kettle and some coffee from the headman. The Sun was just beginning to set, and a large group began to gather around the fire.

I was happy to sit with Bredda Man and the other elders, listening quietly as they teased each other and remembered the day. Everyone laughed heartily.

One of the old men spoke to another elder about his young nephew Munu. Munu was a hard worker and a strong young man.

"Maas Joseph…. What happened to you boy this morning. He looks tired and mawger (thin) like when thunder hits a cat under a pear tree!"

Maas Joseph shook his head, as if he was flustered, and sucked his teeth.

Maas Joseph looked over at Munu and said teasingly, "What happened to you boy, you can't speak up for youself and answer the old fool fool (ignorant) man?"

Everyone was quiet as Munu fidgeted uncomfortably, pretending that he was sulking.

Munu's girlfriend, Agatha, sucked her teeth and poked him to chide him because he was playing dumb.

Munu squirmed, making fun of his own discomfort. "Chu, Agatha... woman, what's wrong with *you*?!"

Agatha laughed, and everyone laughed with her.

The evening's fire was the place where the elders could check up on everyone in the group and find out what the day's work had brought about. Maybe there was bad feeling lurking in a heart. Teasing made sure there were no skeletons hiding that would come out and hurt someone, or all of us, in the field. A dark heart made careless, inattentive hands. Those who could not take teasing were "bad minded" and needed to be worked on by themselves, away from the group. No one wished anyone harm in this circle. No one teased to hurt or shame another. Along with the teasing, there was a lot of affectionate bumping into one another and touching that showed the good heartedness of people's intent.

"So... where is the boy that gives away all his pimento to Bredda Man?!"

I blushed, realizing that it was my turn to be teased. I spoke up, confidently, "Yes, sah, I am here!"

The group went quiet as everyone turned to look at me.

Agatha put her hands on her hips and mimicked me in a funny, squeaky little voice, "Yes, sah, I am here!"

We all laughed hard again.

Bredda Man slapped me on the back, grinning as he shook

his head. Then he said, "My little bredda say he is goin to fix up a house for me next year as well."

Another of the elders joined in, "Rass clate is where you find a friendly white child like that…find one for me too…I want one!"

The old people laughed again, and all of us younger ones thought the old man who swore that way was really funny. We enjoyed being encouraged to laugh respectfully with him.

When the coffee was brewed the elders drank full mugs, while we youngsters each got a small cup, topped up with the frothy milk we had brought from the dairy and stored in shaded, cool water all day. We had honey, too, from a hive that the elders had smoked out in an old tree stump nearby. Through the acrid smoke, they pulled out huge chunks of honeycomb and placed them into a big pan to share out. We chewed the honeycomb like chewing gum until all that was left was the wax.

We were still listening to the old men and women making fun of themselves, telling jokes and stories about their adventures and what they learned from their own elders, when I heard car tires on the gravel road and saw the headlights of my grandfather's car. I jumped up and shouted to him as he drove over the cattle crossing in the gateway. He stopped the car and walked over to the group. Maas Joseph and Bredda Man stood up and shook his hand. Bredda Man gave him a mug of coffee.

One of the old men said, "Maas Jim, where can I find a young white friend like this one to help me?!"

I felt embarrassed because the elder had honored me to make polite conversation with my grandfather.

Grandfather looked proudly at me, "Listen, I had to steal him from his family … after he is done building up my house when I get old, you all can borrow him!"

He acted like he was old and feeble and pretended to be hanging on to me for support. Everyone howled with laughter again. Then my grandfather respectfully sat down on the ground with everyone else, comfortably slipping into the circle as if it was home.

The old man who had sworn, now pretended to fall over, sucking his teeth and shouting "Rass Clate, there is only one of them...friendly white kids. It's true!"

Munu gave me a big smile when the laughter subsided. I felt honored to be teased this way. I knew the teasing was meant to make me strong.

When Grandfather and I said our goodnights, we shook hands respectfully with all the old men before setting off up the hill to have dinner.

Bredda Man came with us and joined us for dinner. He and grandfather talked about the land and what needed to be done. After dinner we sat outside on the porch for a while, and grandfather pointed out the satellites that orbited the Earth, looking like tiny stars moving in a straight line across the horizon.

Before he left Bredda Man asked me to meet him and walk with him to the harvest the next day.

When I finally went to bed I was still full of the wood smoke and the laughter from the fireplace gathering. I fell asleep with the knowing that something important was about to happen in my life.

The next morning after I finished milking the cows, Bredda Man and I set off for the harvest together. I asked him about his artwork. "Bredda Man why do you make carvings and things like that?"

He smiled and said, "It's a way to speak for things that don't have a voice unless we talk for them. When we talk for

Creation, she teaches us things we could never know unless we give her our voice."

I was confused. He looked at me and said, "Come here, maan." I followed him over to the foot of a huge guangu tree.

"You see this tree and you pass him every day. Him whisper and talk to you every day but what him say is so soft you can't hear nor feel it. It stays inside you like secret knowledge, till you use it. You already know things about him that you never going to understand unless you talk for him."

I didn't get it, and Bredda Man saw that I was struggling. "Make me show you what I mean," he said.

Bredda Man looked at the tree and spoke. "Bredda Guangu your roots draw water from deep in the Earth Queen to make your leaves turn green. It's the same roots that draw water into the Earth Queen's body when it rains. It's the same way I am, too, for I, maan, have roots that draw on the waters of imagination and the body of the Earth Queen to nourish my understanding."

As I listened, I was catapulted into a different world. I suddenly realized I was connected to nature in this simple way, and that I had always sensed this but had not voiced, either to myself or others, what Bredda Man had just given words to.

Bredda Man turned to me and asked, "What did you learn from what I said?"

I replied, still in shock and amazement, "I learn say the bush can teach me things."

The words just came out of me, and I felt amazed again.

Bredda Man smiled, "Aiiheee! You see what I, maan, a tell you. The tree talks but not like we talk. So when I talk for the tree I understand something I couldn't know before I spoke.

Now it's your turn to speak for the tree."

I thought hard about what to say. "Tree, you stand up tall and strong and give shade to plenty of people. I want to be like you, too. I want to be big enough to help make other people find peace under my shelter, too." I was surprised at what I had said. Once I started, the words seemed to have a life of their own.

Bredda Man laughed when he saw my shocked expression and then playfully patted me on the back. "You see what happens when you talk for the elders in Creation. Some of us can easily hear what Creation says and teaches. Some of us can't hear anything at all. And in some of us, knowledge is shut up inside so long it gets dark and starts to rot. Then, them who can't hear must feel!"

Bredda Man whipped his fingers purposefully in the air. A shiver ran down my spine. We went on together to the harvest for the day.

When I walked by the tree on the way home, I felt drawn to it again, as if we were friends. In my heart, there was now a definite difference between that tree and all the others around it. I felt an openness and wanted to share myself again, voicing the connection between us. I wanted to see if I could draw out more knowledge the Earth had taught me, which I had buried inside.

But as I stood alone in front of the tree, I felt completely overwhelmed by its huge presence. This tree was now alive on an entirely different level. I could feel it vibrating. I felt it had emotions. I suddenly became disturbed about the warmth I felt toward the tree, and which I felt coming from the tree toward me. I had opened up something my whole being registered, but I couldn't handle it. I decided it was because I was tired and hungry from the day's work, and I needed to go home to eat and rest. I retreated hastily from the tree, telling myself I would try again the next day.

After dinner, when I felt calmer, I thought about what had happened. I realized I had experienced a tremendous shift in my awareness. I had met the tree as if it were a person. My curiosity was ignited, but there was also a hesitancy about fully exploring this new found world. My ego was clinging desparately to walls of fear and doubt, trying to maintain some sense of familiarity.

I had been invited to enter a vast and expansive world, where I could bring teachings from the living world of nature into my understanding. It was not at all what I had been previously taught to think about life and nature. Nature herself, it seemed, had something to teach me, if only I let her speak through me. I had never imagined something like this would come to me. I was at once determined to explore the possibility of speaking again with the natural world, even though I was also still extremely nervous about doing it.

The next morning I was up early. The sky was overcast and the clouds were heavy and low. They smelled like rain. After helping with the cows, I decided to see whether the feeling of warmth would be there again with the guangu tree. As I approached the tree, I was immediately drawn toward it. I felt my heart open. I also began to feel uncomfortable again. I was just about to leave when I saw Bredda Man come walking down the path.

He smiled when he saw me standing by the tree. "What makes us afraid … is when we can't speak for the elements and Creation. Once we start to give them a voice, everything is all right. Everything wants to open to us, same way as the tree. Everything wants to open to us. It's the same way we are, too. When we find somebody who can speak for the things we know, that were buried inside our heart, we feel tallowah (strong and beautiful)!

"When we listen to someone who has great insight and understanding, or someone with a beautiful vision or great faith in something good, we feel inspired and want to open to that person. They speak for those things inside us and we feel more able to feel those things."

I looked up at his eyes and they were full of kindness and a gentle intensity that made me relax. He put his hand on my shoulder and said softly, coaxing me, "It's not that you are afraid of the tree and what you feel, but of what you don't understand. Your heart is not afraid at all. Your heart is full like the clouds. Look at the clouds."

I looked up at the clouds and noticed how full they were, and how dark and ominous some of them seemed.

"What are they telling you?"

"They are telling us it is going to rain soon."

"How does it feel when they tell you something?"

"It feels tense, like they are frightened," I said, already allowing my fear to color the way I perceived the world.

Bredda Man smiled knowingly and looked into my eyes. His smile made me feel very vulnerable and self-conscious, until I started to understand what he was asking me to do.

I realized that speaking for them, instead of acting out my fear, was a whole new way of being alive on the Earth for me.

Bredda Man echoed my knowing. "Maybe if you talk for them it will help them to feel better." He smiled again, suggesting he knew already I would benefit from what he asked.

I looked at the clouds and began to speak. "You are carrying water and it feels heavy and makes you look dark."

As I said what I saw, I realized I was speaking about my own heart and the feelings I carried inside, like rain clouds, ready to burst out. I felt my heart flutter, because I had taken a risk in showing what I was feeling.

I continued to voice my seeing, "My heart carries feelings just like you clouds. I was afraid of the feelings the tree has. But I understand my own dark clouds of fear have to burst before I can know the feelings of others."

As soon as I began to give a voice to my inner state, I felt a fresh breeze blowing through the bush.

With a big, proud smile on his face, Bredda Man motioned me to continue.  I felt a lot lighter. I noticed that my heart, which had been fearful before, was now clear and bright. I felt a huge sense of relief.

I decided to try to speak for the wind. "Wind, your blowing through the bush and touching everything makes everything feel clean and peaceful, just like my voice when I speak about my feelings inside, I feel clean and fresh, too."

The moment I finished speaking, the dark clouds broke, releasing their rain. We ran to shelter under some trees.

I felt completely different now. Awake to the elements and living world around me. I felt the whole forest open to me. I was standing on holy ground beside a strange but beautiful being that I had known for an eternity. I looked into Bredda Man's eyes and saw reflected the same knowing that I was feeling. We smiled together in recognition of our hearts being open to all of life.

The peace and beauty in that moment was incredible and yet perfectly familiar … as if I had known this feeling all along, but had simply set it aside. I was perfectly at peace in this state and with Bredda Man. He spoke quietly as we watched the last of the rain shower dance across the leaves on the ground.

"That is the voice of ancient human being, little bredda, that is the voice of human being."

As we walked toward the harvest circle, the ground shimmered with puddles. Droplets of water glittered everywhere. I imagined Heaven was in the Earth and the Earth was adorned with moist, sparkling jewels. I imagined that nature knew every part of my being and I accepted this feeling.

Within a deep silence in my heart, I heard myself thinking, "I belong on the Earth. This is my home."

I felt Bredda Man listening to what I was feeling and thinking. I said, "When I speak for the elements and Creation, I learn something. Is that always so?"

Bredda Man made a face and teased me, "I surely don't know, sah!"

Then he looked more serious. "It's something that only comes with practice. Each and every day, if you speak for the elements and Creation, you will surely grow wise."

I looked at Bredda Man. He was confident in himself, but in a very unassuming way. I promised to speak for the animals and plants, the clouds and elements, each and every day.

"I feel I must grow wise if I practice every day.... I will learn so much!"

Bredda Man laughed, his shoulders bobbing up and down as he chuckled.

When we reached the gathering place, he lit a fire and took his place among the harvest group, while I went to find more bush and cow patties that had not been soaked by the rain.

The days passed quickly. At the end of the summer I returned home to Kingston. My next meeting with Bredda Man would be a turning point in my life.

# 1

# The Lizard's Lesson

I GREW UP in a family of mixed racial and cultural backgrounds. My father's family was from a line of European Jews. My mother's line was also Jewish, with African and Native American mixed in for flavor. My family was wealthy and owned a farm in the hills of Kingston, where my father bred horses and sold real estate. My mother stayed home and played hostess for his frequent entertainment functions. Like many well-to-do, established Jamaican families, we had live-in workers who became part of our family. This had its good points, but also some bad points, as allowances were made for these "family" members that would not have been otherwise tolerated.

CeCe was built like a running back, short and stocky, and had the face of a veteran boxer who had engaged one too many hard-hitting opponents. I always felt she was uncomfortable in a woman's body. CeCe was our cook and baby-sitter. She was also the source of violence toward me that often drove me to seek solace in the woods and countryside.

I was in the outdoor kitchen one time with CeCe. A rat had jumped across the bamboo grove onto the rafters underneath the zinc roof and was taking a shortcut through the kitchen to get onto another roof. That poor rat should have known better than to cross over the roof beams of CeCe's kitchen. Bad mistake!

CeCe had been calmly doing the dishes when she saw the rat scurrying across the rafter. In a flash, she rolled up her wet dishcloth, side-stepped, and hurled the cloth at the rat. Before the rat even hit the floor, CeCe had jumped into the air and, in the same moment as it landed, she came down and crushed its head with her bare foot. Afterward, I carried the broken, dead rat body outside and put it up on a high fence post by the horse pens to feed the John Crows. When a big John Crow approached it and began tearing the skin off the rat's limp frame, I remember thinking as I watched, hypnotized, that the rat had served a good purpose in feeding that noble bird.

All of us kids were awed by CeCe's ferocity and precision, and, as you can imagine, we were afraid of her. We were especially afraid of her when she was drunk.

CeCe loved to drink rum—a Jamaican "tradition" that is steeped in the sugar cane plantation days of slavery. She drank white rum, which is especially strong stuff. It is used as medicine for rubbing sore joints and preserving teas and herbs. When she got drunk, CeCe would beat us with a big bamboo stick that she hid behind an armchair in our bedroom. It seemed that although rum is fondly spoken of as a "spirit healer," it also fuels the suppressed violence of Jamaica's unwilling native population against the dictates of a rigid and oppressive culture.

My parents did not know about these beatings because we were afraid to tell on CeCe. And there, anyway, wouldn't have been much safety in telling them because my parents, like many other Jamaican parents, thought a beating was the best thing for most of what ails children. And so, I spent as much time as possible away from home, hunting and trapping in the hills and mountains around Kingston.

One day, I was coming back from a hunting trip up in the mountains when I met Bredda Man. He seemed to know about a maniacal preoccupation I had—shooting lizards, and especially the big green ones.

He asked me, "Remember how you learned to speak for Creation under the guangu tree the first time?"

I nodded.

He went on. "Violence and killing is what happens when we are afraid to communicate and bring out what drives us … nobody can understand us then … it's like a bad dream we can't remember … that dream makes us feel bad all day, even if we can't remember it."

When Bredda Man said this I became thoughtful and defensive. Then Bredda Man said he wanted to show me something and asked me to follow him.

We walked into a field where my dad kept some of his horses. There were about fifty guava trees, laden with sweet, syrupy fruit. Grass quits, pitchairies, logger heads, john chewits, blue tits, and auntie katies were all feasting on the ripe, yellow guavas. The air was filled with the buzz of wasps and hornets, which especially loved to build their nests in these trees. The Sun was high in a deep crystalline blue sky. The smell of the ripe guavas and the honey-scented wild flowers in the tall grass was intoxicating. They seemed to whisper to me, and I began to think of how I had often played in this field with other children.

Sometimes we hid up in the guava trees, holding clotheslines ready until the horses came to eat the fruit, then we lassoed the horses and rode them bareback with a makeshift halter. We also climbed the huge mango tree on the ridge of the hill nearby and danced on its limbs until the soft, small fruits rained down, striking the Earth like galloping hooves. Then we filled boxes and boxes with mangos. We sometimes ate so much on the way home that we had to go back and pick more, so we would have plenty to give away at home.

I was enjoying my pleasant reverie when I suddenly felt the air around me become still and stifling. I came back with a jolt to the present. Bredda Man was singing softly and rubbing his sweat over his arms, chest and face. I started to pay attention and felt a presence begin to grow stronger around us. Bredda Man's body seemed to be charged with an immense energy field. I had a sense that something important was about to happen.

The look of intent on his face was calm but intense. He hummed and sang softly as he approached one of the guava trees. Then he swiftly and smoothly reached in and plucked out a huge hornets' nest—just as if it were a ripe fruit. The wasps swarmed and crawled all over his hands and arms, but they didn't bite him.

I felt quiet and perfectly at ease. It was as if some power that was truly peaceful filled my being. In a state of suspended animation, I watched the wasps wander harmlessly over Bredda Man. Then he carefully and reverently placed the nest back among the branches.

This was not a ceremonious event. Bredda Man made it look simple and sweet. He was merely showing me something that he knew would help me attend to what he wanted to teach me. I knew he had worked hard to learn how to do what he had just performed so effortlessly. Something deep inside me connected with his training and dedication to such a gentle, respectful relationship with nature.

Slowly coming out of my state of awe, I began to rationalize inwardly what I had just witnessed. But Bredda Man spoke to me while I was still in my state of grace, "What shadow of fear covers your heart and makes you hate your bredda lizard so much? You forgot already … the Earth Queen wouldn't hurt you. No matter what the lizard did, and you forgot…. It's a teaching, he was teaching you. It doesn't make sense to kill him because he is giving you a gift to teach you. Lizard is teaching you about the forgotten dreams and memories that drive us like slaves. Lizard chose you, to give his gift to! He is calling to you, so you will awaken the knowledge inside and remember."

Bredda Man's words were echoing in my head as we walked back to the road. I was fully awake now, and I heard every syllable clearly as if he were repeating it over and over again. The road suddenly seemed strange. I felt dazed and lost. Then the words started to subside and I heard a ringing in my ears. I began to feel a little dizzy, so I sat down on the bank by the side of the road.

Bredda Man sat down beside me and started to tell me a story. It was an old Ananci story. At first his voice seemed far-away, "One time, Ananci was king over a whole jungle...."

I felt as if I was drifting in and out of a daydream as I listened to Bredda Man tell the story:

Ananci has two children, but a wicked chief cursed his wife when the children were young, so Ananci raises them up alone. The girl child is dark and soft and her name is Baihema. The boy, he is light and hard, and he is named Maiyeh.

One day they see an ugly hag asleep in the forest. Her name is Damah. Whenever she wakes up, all she can do is curse Ananci, and say "I am looking for the wicked *ginal* (trickster) King Ananci." The children never tell her, Ananci is their father. So they mislead her and she goes on about her business. They are lucky because every time Damah falls asleep, she forgets what she was doing and who she met last time she was awake.

But Maiyeh is afraid to go out in the forest again after meeting Damah and he locks himself up inside his room. Baihema feels angry because she has to do all the chores. Now she feels bad against her brother as she struggles to finish his work as well as her own. Then she gets even more bad tempered when she remembers that her brother is hiding in a room where she can't reach him.

Ananci hears about his kids acting fool fool. So he dresses up as if he is the wicked queen and he tricks Baihema to go into the dark room where Maiyeh is hiding. Ananci locks them both up together in the room. Once Baihema is locked up inside with Maiyeh, they both feel sorry for each other. They stop feeling bad about one another. They escape together. As soon as they escape, they chase down the wicked queen, who is Ananci in disguise.

They catch Ananci and tear off his disguise to reveal their father. But then they feel ashamed that they treated their father badly. Ananci has great patience and Wisdom. He could be gentle even though the kids treated him rough. Meantime Ananci tells them he had to trick them to bring them together. They feel better. Ananci warns them about Damah. He tells them the only way to overcome her is to do two things. The first one is to make her stay awake till she can remember their names. After that, if they throw her in the river, all her power will vanish and she can't hurt any-body again.

When the two children feel better, they meet Damah again. This time, they try to trick Damah. They want her to pay attention to them so she can learn their names. They take her on a long walk. Every time she wants to fall asleep they frighten her and shout one of their names out loud and she jumps. "What makes you shout out the names, Baihema and Maiyeh so loudly?" she asks them. Then she mumbles their names, softer and softer, till she forgets them again. Then as her head starts to drop down, they yell their names again. "Maiyeh... Baihema!"

Damah jumps up, awake again, and begins to remember a little more each time she wakes up and is fooled into repeating their names. After a while she starts to call out their names loud and strong like she remembers something important. Her anger toward Ananci grows stronger, too, as she starts to remember. The two children lead her to a river where they tell her she will find Ananci.

When they reach the river Baihema tells Damah to call out her name and Ananci will come out of the river. Damah repeats Baihema's name till she knows it by heart. Then Maiyeh jumps up and shouts, "Its only one of our names you remember… if you don't remember both names and call them out, Ananci won't come out so you can knock him down." So Damah starts to call out the boy's name, too, "Maiyeh … Maiyeh … Maiyeh … Maiyeh!"

Damah calls and calls out till she can remember both of the children's names. When the kids realize she remembers their names, they are no longer afraid of Damah. They grab hold of her and fling her into the river where she swallows a lot of water. Then Damah loses all her power to hurt people and she promises never to hurt them or their father again. Maiyeh and Baihema help her—because she can't swim—Maiyeh helps her out of the water and Baihema cleans her up.

When she gets out of the river she remembers everything. She remembers she was Ananci's queen once upon a time and she remembers she was the mother of the two children until a curse turned her into an old hag and took her away from her family and made her forget everything. Maiyeh and Baihema are surprised and happy to hear her story and find their mother. They take her to their father.

Ananci recognizes her straight away. Now everybody feels good with Ananci, and they listen to what he has to say. Ananci tells the children each of them has a new name. He gives Baihema the name Zamar. He gives Maiyeh the name Shemesh. Ananci shows them the stars and the web of life, and they become wise.

Bredda Man looked at me while I pondered the story. He lit a shag. He puffed on it to get it going, and then he explained, "Everything in the story means something. Maiyeh is hiding in a dark room. Maiyeh represents our young heart of wisdom. Maiyeh made Baihema work extra hard and feel a strain every day. That is what happens when the heart is locked up because of fear or forgetting. The body knows only violence. Baihema represents our body and physical work.

"When we bury something in our heart, our body feels it. Our body has to act it out like a mule until we remember what it is. The body always has to work harder when the heart is fearful and locked up in darkness. That is what Baihema means. Baihema is a dumb beast. This name speaks of the inability to remember and communicate consciously.

"But the body shows everyone else through our posture that we feel sad or angry, tense or relaxed inside. A person may not really ever know this is what others see. Maiyeh is the heart. Damah is the imagination. It's our imagination that tells the heart and the body, 'Our father, our ancient inherent wisdom, is to be feared.'"

Bredda Man looked at me seriously, rubbing his chin, and asked, "You read about wisdom. Tell me who in your schooling and history books, you know as wise?"

I immediately thought about the prophets from the Bible who were the formative archetypal characterizations of wisdom for many Jamaicans. "The prophets and saints?" I replied, with more of a question than an answer. Bredda Man smiled in a friendly, teasing way, squinting up his eyes and face to gently mock my timid answer.

Then he asked, "So what type of life you know the prophets had? How do your teachers talk bout Heaven and God?"

I remembered that most of the stories were violent and most of the words the prophets recorded were harsh and critical. So I replied, "They always talk about hellfire and brimstone, and the prophets call on God to destroy the unbelievers a lot."

Bredda Man nodded his head and asked, seriously, "So what does that tell you about the relationship between prophets and the people?"

I answered immediately, without thinking, "It means the prophets couldn't talk to them because the people were afraid and locked up their hearts until they turned violent." As soon as I spoke, the immensity of what I had said dawned on me.

Bredda Man chuckled mischievously at my report. He took a draw on his shag and then spoke softly, "That is the reason…. All a we fear wisdom. It's rooted in violence, according to those who write history. But the prophets were also sweet and spoke for Creation…with great beauty also.

"But that is not what the people who write history remember. When people can't feel the beauty in the Earth and they can't speak for Creation, everything looks rotten.

"When our hearts are locked up we imagine all kind of wickedness is waiting for us if we dare to take a risk, to speak or even hint at what we feel. Now, many people believe television is the real world and that it teaches us wisdom. The people that write the stories for television don't understand our simple life. When people watch television long enough they begin to believe our simple life is no longer as real as what they see on the television.

"Nor do they understand the sweetness and peace of the Earth's wisdom. It's the same thing as the people who write history. To this day, wisdom is presented as a frightening and violent power! What we imagine is true is only an illusion.

That is the trick Damah plays in the story, telling everyone that the wisdom of Ananci is violent.

"That is what happens to the power of imagination when it goes to sleep, when it has no true connection to the past and it can't speak for Creation. History is like Damah; it can only remember what happens when it is awake. When our heart fears wisdom, we hold back because it is frightening to accept the most sacred teachings and knowledge Creation gives us. That is when Baihema has to work all by herself because Maiyeh is locked up in darkness. Whenever our true heart holds back, our body suffers. We work like a dumb beast, without knowing why we are violent and hurt Creation.

"It's only when wisdom tricks us into facing our fears, that we can set our heart free and stop damaging our body by making it work as a dumb beast. Ananci, the symbol of wisdom, has to trick the emotions and the body into working together again. When we look inside to accept and face our fears, we are locked up in fearful dark introspection, like Ananci locked up the two children.

"Just like you and the lizard … your heart is locked up because of fear. You can't remember when the fear started to hold on to you. When you take the fear you have and speak for the lizard, you will remember the first time you were afraid. Then your heart will be free.

"I am like Ananci, tricking your body and heart to listen and seek out the memory that makes you hate the lizard so much. When you start to look inside and speak for the lizard in Creation … then you throw imagination into the clean flowing river of the living heart ... and you remember everything.

"That's when we start to understand instead of being fearful. We remember what happened to make us afraid. Imagination starts to work for our healthfulness instead of our illusions. Then imagination, Damah, becomes the companion and wife of wisdom, and our hearts become the friend and brother to our body and all Creation."

Bredda Man smiled and looked at me piercingly. "That is why Maiyeh becomes Shemesh … Shemesh means Sun. There is no greater friend to Creation than the Sun. Baihema becomes Zamar. Zamar is to dance. When we can bring the fears into our speaking for Creation … our body changes from a burdened mule to a dancer. Everything becomes a dance and we move with life instead of like a slave … against life."

I was amazed at how much knowledge was contained in such a short story. I was struggling to absorb even a fraction of what I had heard. "What a great story," I exclaimed.

"It's in your heart that your fear of your bredda lizard is locked up. To go back to the heart, you have to ask your bredda lizard to help you. When your heart is locked up in the darkness of fear, you will imagine wisdom is a demon and you will believe ugliness is the face of the most sacred beauty."

Then Bredda Man said something that almost knocked me over. "The wisdom you fear is a teaching you have learned that imagination interprets as, 'We *rule* the animals!' Listen to me, little bredda, 'To rule truly, is to serve.'"

When he said those words, I felt his intent going through my spirit like a comb untying knots and twisted strands. "To rule truly, is to serve."

Bredda Man continued, "You believe that we are masters of Creation. It is a teaching we all learn by example. How can there be uncaring and cruelty in true mastery? In your heart your fear of the lizard is locked up because of this confustion. But the only knowledge we truly have is what we have experienced ourselves, inside and around us."

I felt a release. Bredda Man was right … I had believed I could hurt the lizards and it would not matter because I was their master. I suddenly felt very vulnerable.

"Let me ask you another question," he said.

I followed his gaze as he looked away to the hills. We watched a dark cloud moving into the valley toward us. Then he turned to me with a very gentle expression on his face and asked, "When they teach you to learn addition and subtraction in school, you are learning how to master the human world, that is how it goes?"

I nodded my head, agreeing, because without math, we could not survive in our society.

"So the greatest mathematicians and masters of geometry are feared and reviled by everyone?"

I was confused. Why would the greatest masters of math be feared? I was beginning to think, with a twinge of irritation, that Bredda Man didn't really understand the modern world that I was growing up in.

"Mastery of the animals is built upon the fact that we disrespect and abuse them, however we please. Isn't this the same way the master of slaves interprets mastery? So this interpretation directs us to believe, mastery of math should mean that we are going to use what we know to steal from and mislead the ignorant!"

Bredda Man stopped to check my astonished face.

I had been lured into a sense of arrogant security and I had tripped up on my own assumptions. I felt ashamed of my thought that Bredda Man was just an uneducated country man.

He smiled compassionately and asked me, "When you learn to swim and master the water, is it because you are going to drown people, or is it so you can enjoy the water?"

"To enjoy the water." I replied cautiously.

Bredda Man looked at me attentively and said, "Then you see how this wisdom is turned upside down. When wisdom is twisted up like this, it makes us afraid to think about it. When we keep our knowing separate from our heart and conscience we feel a great sadness and loneliness inside. Mastery is just like the rain, when it falls it doesn't just fall on one person's roof."

Bredda Man had shown me something about my own conditioning that was a festering wound in my spirit. There was a huge gap between the meaning I had assumed for "mastery" in my head which could not be reconciled with my heart. I had never questioned this before. Now I was feeling totally vulnerable and open.

Bredda Man went on, "We believe we are human 'masters' of Creation. In the way we have been taught to apply mastery, that means you can abuse your bredda lizard without your heart opening. Not feeling anything protects that teaching. Our wisdom becomes a boundary line when we use it this way.

"But listen, little bredda, our compassionate, living heart doesn't know any boundary lines. Our heart doesn't only feel our own joy and suffering, it feels all Creation's joys and suffering. It can't stay inside no fence.

"When we develop understanding we entrust the fences of thinking that we have learned to the vast heartland of Creation. With understanding we begin to heal the separation of these teachings from the vastness of the living heart. It is not easy to move from the safety of the fences we have learned into the wilderness of the living heart, little bredda. Without understanding there can be no trust. Understand the lizard's gift, little bredda, and move into the living heart."

Bredda Man looked at me very tenderly, seeing the fear and doubts that clouded my heart. He watched me checking to see if I would hear more. I wanted to hear what he said.

He continued in a gentle voice, "Most people's fear comes from knowing the fences of thinking we learned will not survive in the vastness of our living heart. The same fear we have of mastery is fear of our own self … as a circle … as wholeness within Creation.

"In the story, Damah is afraid of Ananci, the one who tricks us into moving beyond our fences of learning to experience the living heart. That is the truth of knowing the whole story is inside all of us. When we balance the wisdom we have learned with our living heart, we create understanding. Our understanding heals the separation our fences build up.

"Every character in the story is part of our circle of wholeness. Every story is the same story. Every dream is the same teaching. We are part of a wholeness and our thoughts and feelings can work to heal that wholeness. It takes a long time to know we can use this healing in our life and Creation, little bredda.

Damah had to remember the names of the children over and over. This is how we train ourselves to understand. We learn through repetition. We learn in simple ways, maaan. When we work consistently to remember and heal our wholeness, we bring all the aspects of our circle together in balance with Creation. This is true mastery, little bredda … yes maaan … this is the teaching of the Earth Queen.

Remember, when Ananci and Damah and the children came together the story was complete. The children entered the dance of life. When we heal the wounds of separation, we know the beauty of the living heart as the center of our circle and we dance with our teachers, no matter whether they are darkness or light."

Bredda Man looked at me again. His words had touched something deep inside and I felt like crying. I was ashamed because I felt I had failed in so many ways. I had assumed so much that now, from listening to Bredda Man, I realized was foolish. I could see the fence I had built that made it safe for me to cruelly hunt the lizards, but I did not know if I could go beyond its confines. Bredda Man stood up. I felt more tense than ever. He turned to me and said, "Now, Ananci, lock up Baihema and Maiyeh together. … Let us see how they get on together!"

I suddenly understood what he meant. I was in the story!

Then he tosseled my hair, teasing me, and said, "Everything all right, little bredda, everything alright…. There is only one love, my little bredda … there is only one love.

As I watched Bredda Man walk away, I wanted to call out to him and apologize. I wanted to throw a rock at him. I wanted to smash a lizard for causing all this frustration in me. Instead, dazed and confused, I turned and walked slowly toward home.

I wasn't at all on the same path I walked down before. My body felt alive and full of excitement, terror, anguish, joy. I knew that I stood at a crossroad in my being. I realized this was the first time I had seen how the source of my fears was determined by the way I thought about something. I could feel the power of knowing that my thoughts conditioned my fears and emotions. And now I could choose this inner world.

This would be an awesome road to walk in life. It loomed up in front of me like a giant wave before an inexperienced surfer. But it was not the wave that was terrifying … it was the choice itself—to take it, to go for it and ride it—knowing that once I had learned to ride the big wave, the smaller ones would never be terrifying—or satisfying—again.

I was comfortable with the small waves in my life. I related well to the other people in my life because they too feared the tiny waves of power. Now I could choose to interpret wisdom so that I would live in peace, rather than fear, with Creation and surf the giant power in life. But choosing the big wave, taking this inner path, seemed a lonely path to walk. None of my old assumptions and expectations in life were safe anymore.

I could still feel Bredda Man watching me, silently reminding me about the lizards. I was scared to think about choosing to return to the source of the lizard's gift. I was scared to heal my interpretation of mastery in the face of my fears.

Back at home, the terror gradually subsided. But, though the natural world had always been a source of great reverence and awe to me as I grew up in Jamaica and though Bredda Man's words haunted me, I hunted the dreaded lizards more than ever before.

Bredda Man's words had sparked an intense panic in me that I could not understand. I spent more and more time trying to shut them out, but the more I tried to shut them out, the more they brought to the surface a strange and helpless rage.

# 2

# The Lizard's Gift

I WAS WALKING back from one of my lizard hunting trips, down the riverbed of a huge natural gully by the dirt road that led to my house. The sides of the gully were steep and the Sun hardly peeked through the overgrown foliage and tall trees that covered the high ridge.

Bredda Man was waiting for me. He was sitting on a stone wall, smoking his shag. The tobacco's strong sweet smell wafted through the damp air, telling me he was watching me. I knew he had seen me shooting lizards again. I felt exposed and nervous. I wanted to run away and hide, but instead, I just stood there, stiff as a board.

I was not surprised to see that his face was cold and hard. I was aware that we were alone in the bush, and I suddenly felt scared. His dark eyes penetrated into my soul, but when he spoke it was with a sad, gentle voice. "Is how you can still kill your bredda lizard and how you can not respect your heart?" I had expected anger, but his gentleness was even more powerful. I heard what he said as if it was my own heart speaking. I did not know how to answer his question. My heart started to beat very fast.

He went on. "Are you hungry? ... Is it hunger? ... why you are killing the lizards?"

I lowered my head and shook it.

"So you not going to eat them, you not going to listen to what your heart tells you.... nor respect it ... and you are not going to hear what I, maan, says either?" I was unable to answer because I felt very ashamed. I knew that it was not a good-hearted thing to kill and not eat one's prey.

Then Bredda Man said something that baffled me. He said it in a strange tone of voice that made it seem like a news report.

"Haven't you heard, whenever you kill lizards...your slingshot will break?"

I thought what he said was silly. Why hadn't my slingshot broken when I had shot lizards up until now? I made an excuse to leave and walked away, feeling not at all sure we were still friends.

I was suddenly feeling tired, so I lay down to rest on the grass under a large guava tree. When I opened my eyes again, I was staring straight up at a huge green lizard on the branch directly above me. I grabbed my slingshot and took aim.... there was a resounding "craaack!"... the entire crook of the slingshot had split in two. One side flew over my hand and flopped about uselessly.

I was completely baffled. I had never seen a slingshot crook snap like that before. My knuckles were red and sore where the crook had whacked them. How absurd! So, not only had Bredda Man's prophecy come true, but I also got a slap on the knuckles while I was proving it! Not about to let myself think that Bredda Man was right, I went and immediately cut another crook.

I soon found another lizard. I took aim, but before I could let the "tongue" go, I felt a gentle tickling on my wrist. The rubber tie that held the leather tongue in place had unwound itself. The tongue had split. Now I was really frustrated. I wasn't going to let a ridiculous "bush prophecy" get the better of me … no siree. Who did Bredda Man think he was, telling me my slingshot will break!

That night I thought about what had happened. Something wasn't right. I started to feel scared. Maybe I would lay off killing lizards for a while. That seemed less of a challenge than trying to understand why all of a sudden my slingshot kept breaking every time I shot at one.

However, the next day I rebuilt my slingshot and went off hunting again. When I finally spotted a lizard, I double-checked my slingshot before I put the river stone into the tongue. This time I wasn't shooting at the lizard just because I was angry with it. Now I had to establish control over my own fate and overthrow Bredda Man's "curse."

I took aim confidently and pulled the rubber way back to make sure I could get a good strong shot off. Plap! The rubber broke! I threw the slingshot down on the ground in disgust and cursed it for its loyalty to Bredda Man, and for betraying my faith in it.

I was frustrated because I knew something was happening that I did not understand, and I knew Bredda Man was the only one who could explain it to me. I was too annoyed at first to face him, but then I decided I would talk to him about it when I saw him again.

The next day, when I saw Bredda Man on the way to the harvest, I asked, "Why can't I shoot lizards, Bredda Man?"

Bredda Man thought for a long while, and when he finally spoke, he said gently, "It's because in your heart you know what I say is true…. It's as simple as that…. Lizard is your bredda and your teacher. It's time for you to speak for them instead of killing them. Listen to your heart and what they want to teach you.

"It's not for you to kill lizards any more! Now your imagi-nation has to learn a new way to see lizards. You have a gift the lizard brings to you. Its time to accept this gift and the responsibility for it. If you see them, ask them to forgive you for the harm you have done to their children and their families. And don't ever joke about this, for it's a serious thing! Ask your lizard brothers to help you to remember the gifts they have to give you. You remember the story bout Maiyeh and Baihema?" I nodded.

"You have to go back into the dark room where your heart is alone and afraid." He looked at me intensely and was silent. I knew there was nothing more to say. I would stop killing lizards.

Some weeks later, I was out in the field picking mangoes for my mother. The number eleven mangoes are small and stringy, but really sweet and juicy. As I stood up in the tree, some horses came underneath and patiently waited for me to drop a few down.

I climbed down to feed the horses a few of the mangoes by hand, holding them carefully in the flat of my hands with my fingers all tightly pressed together. Horse's lips have a way of dragging bent fingers in between their powerful teeth. It is a real challenge not to get an "equestrian manicure." They take the whole mango into their mouth and then plop out the seed as they chew up the rest, juice dripping out of the corners of their mouth. Underneath the tree was full of the dried out seeds and skins discarded over the whole season.

I was about to take my box of mangoes home when I saw a huge iguana on a limb in a guava tree nearby. He was watching me intently. Instinctively, I looked for a stick to attack the big lizard, but then I remembered Bredda Man's words.

I struggled to gather my thoughts and feelings. All I could hear was "dumb beast," going through my head, from the Ananci story. It was useless to fight Bredda Man... and my heart did not want to … only my arrogance did. This time, I was determined that my true and peaceful heart was going to win. I made myself sit down beneath the tree.

As soon as I sat down, the same terror I felt when Bredda Man first spoke to me about the lizards, came back. Then I began to remember the story, about going into the dark room to face my heart, Maiyeh. I felt good—for a moment—remembering the bright part of me that was locked away. The lizard watched me carefully, rolling his eyes to see where he could jump for safety. Staring back into the lizard's eyes, I felt terrified again. Something ancient in his eyes challenged me to enter a different world than I had ever been in before.

The lizard did not move. I summoned up my courage and decided to try what Bredda Man had suggested. I started to talk to the lizard. "Lizard, I am really sorry I hurt you and your family...." Before I had finished my thought, I felt tears well up in my eyes. I was overwhelmed with tremendous waves of grief. The emotion I felt seemed way out of proportion to the small gesture I had just made. Then, as part of me watched, unmoved, my body cleansed itself of fear. I sobbed uncontrollably. My chest heaved and my body shuddered. All of a sudden, the shuddering stopped. I was not scared any more. I looked up. The lizard was observing me calmly. He looked at me as if he had known all along I would be coming and that I would not hurt him. I felt peaceful. Why had I feared him? The lizard was lying there with his eyes half closed. I felt that he was dreaming about us together there.

I heard Bredda Man's words, "Talk for the lizard so your heart can be free." I remembered how I had first talked for the guangu tree and the clouds. Since then I had practiced many times speaking for the rivers, stones, plants, and trees. I remembered my experiences and was determined to try to speak for the lizard.

As I watched the lizard, the words slowly came out of me, "You keep the guava tree clean by eating the insects. I, too, can be useful to the trees and healthy ways of being in my world. When I choose to give Creation a voice, I am being useful the same as you. I feed on the little creeping fears and doubts that will bore into the tree of my heart." I was astonished by what I had said, and the meaning surprised me.

I thought back to when I had experienced the subtle switch—when the huge wave loomed up in front of me.... Now I was surfing a big wave at last. I had chosen to face the source of my fears and assumptions instead of acting them out with violence.... I could talk my fears into the world instead of letting them drive me. The realization I had earlier made sense now. I sat there for some time, dreamily enveloped in the elation of my discovery.

"Maybe the lizard is the one that helped me to understand things." I said out loud. I looked back at the lizard again. He was calm and unmoving. I felt the lizard was connecting me to a deeper reality. He seemed to be broadcasting what I felt and said to the entire forest, through some telepathic psychic network. Somehow this being was the doorway into my own healing and my experience of the wholeness of Creation.

I remembered what Bredda Man said about mastery. I felt I was healing the wound of separation that I had created by applying mastery only to the human world. In healing this simple meaning, I felt I had taken a big step toward healing the way I used my intelligence. I told my self that now my mind was whole and that my understanding applied to all Creation in the same way. It all seemed so simple then, but later I would realize what a profound decision I had made.

A dark shadow had been removed from my heart. My heart was full of joy toward the lizard now. I hoped that I would be forgiven for all the damage I had done to his family because of my mysterious rage.

As I sat and watched the old Lizard, I started to feel a kinship with him. I wondered what I could offer to the lizard to show him I meant well. Suddenly, I remembered to ask what his gift to me was. I asked nervously, and, for a while, the lizard remained, quietly listening.

Then he suddenly came vividly alive. His whole demeanor changed. He became intensely powerful. He glared at me, and I was filled with fear again. I felt a charge of energy move from his eyes into mine. Then I was surfing a big wave again, speaking for Creation. "This fear you bring me is a next big wave to speak for … to surf on and know wisdom." In that moment, I knew I was the lizard's true friend and no longer an enemy to my own wisdom. I felt a strange churning inside as the terror and helplessness turned into excitement and release.

Then, slowly and methodically, the lizard turned and moved away. Like some ancient dinosaur that knew his work was done, he carefully left me to ponder the immensity of what we had shared.

As I watched the lizard climb slowly upward and disappear into the dark green foliage, I felt a bond with him beyond anything I had imagined was possible. I could not shake the feeling of what I had seen in the glaring eyes of that powerful being. I left feeling uneasy, but with a sense of completion.

I carried the box of mangoes home and tried to forget about the uneasiness I felt when I was held in the lizard's gaze.

Before I went to sleep that night, I thought about the story of Maiyeh and Baihema again and again. Each time, more of it came alive. I couldn't believe I was so caught up in this simple Ananci story, and that it seemed so powerful to me. I couldn't think about anything else. It was as if I was becoming part of the story.

I was sure about the understanding I had gained through the window of the story. I had gone into the dark room to meet the heart that was scared—my own. My imagination and my heart had come together to speak for Creation, and together we saw our escape. Yet, I knew there was something missing, but I could not put my finger on it. My heart was free to stop holding back anymore and I could trust the forest and the lizards again. Well ... almost. I was already beginning to doubt that the gift I got from the lizard was a good one.

The next part of the story was about finding the wicked queen who frightened my heart into hiding away. I thought about my imagination and how my heart and body could find the secret that was hidden in the darkness of imagination. As I was trying to figure out how I would solve the secret of the story in my imagination, I drifted off to sleep, still hanging on to the vague feeling of being a part of the story.

Sometime during the night I woke up crying and afraid. I had dreamed I was an infant and that a large iguana bit me on the crown of the head.

Now I remembered everything.... In my dream I was lying in a crib at my aunt's house. I looked outside the window and saw a large green iguana staring at me. I remember the same ancient glare in his eyes. I had an ominous feeling as the iguana climbed down the tree and out of sight. Then I felt something come from behind and nip the hair on top of my head and pin me to the floor of the crib. I could not speak words, so I shrieked as I struggled to free myself. I remember hearing footsteps, and then feeling my body recoil as if I had been suddenly released. I rolled over to see the green iguana looking back, smiling, as he sauntered out the door.

When my mother finally came, try as I might I could not explain, because I could not speak. I remember being frustrated and crying hysterically.

municate my fear. It wasn't about the lizard at all…it was about my feeling of being unable to communicate my fear.

This was the reason I had been hunting the lizards for so long! I was shocked by the realization that something that happened to me so long ago could drive me to such blind rage and insensitivity for so many years. And I didn't even know it! This deeply buried memory had driven me for years to act out its forgotten imperative. I was controlled by a hypnotic rage that was triggered every time I saw a lizard. I suddenly thought, "Perhaps everyone experiences things they can't remember that make them act badly."

I could hardly think because the realization was so over-whelming for me. That's what Bredda Man knew all along! That's why he helped me to learn to speak for Creation and my fear. Bredda Man had given me the exact antidote for my poisonous rage at being unable to express my fear and knowledge—talking for Creation.

Life suddenly became a flowing force inside me. I let go of my fear. I was the river now, flowing freely, not the one who was afraid of change any more. Then another realization hit me. I had found the wicked queen, the part imagination had played in the drama of the memory. I remembered the lizard's momentous gift as an attack, I saw wisdom as a bad or fearful power that made me into a helpless victim.

Seeing how I had interpreted what happened had made my life a limited walk of fearful doubt and anger. Choosing to see the lizard's gift as a powerful awakening changed every-thing. I felt like I had taken my first step into Bredda Man's world. Something in me woke up. Something deep inside lit up and started to shine.

I wanted to wake up my parents and talk to them. I ran excitedly to their door and was about to knock, but then I remembered they had no idea what was going on, and besides, it was four o'clock in the morning. As I went back to my bed, I felt lonely. I had learned something incredible, and I wanted to tell the world, but I couldn't. No one in my family would ever believe me. And I realized something even more disheartening, it resounded with crystal clarity in my heart, "No one else will even care."

I remembered the story again, and how Ananci taught the heart, imagination, and body about the stars. I felt this bright understanding inside me was just like one of the stars in the story. This sparkling understanding lit up my inner world's sky with a feeling of joy deep inside my being. Then I remembered that there was someone I could tell who would understand—Bredda Man!

I could hardly wait to see him again, to tell him about the lizard's gift to me and ask if I had truly understood the story.

At the crack of dawn I ran down to Bredda Man's cabin. He was in his garden, cleaning out dried up leaves from the sugar cane and banana plants. First he showed me how to cut down the banana trees that had already borne fruit. He explained how the new ones would grow up from the old ones that were laid down. Then he showed me how to plant sugar cane in the rich fertile soil and how to hang the huge flat leaves of the tobacco plants upside down on a line to dry in the Sun.

Finally, after we finished the work, I had a chance to tell him about my discoveries.

Before I spoke, Bredda Man smiled with a mischievous grin, "What makes you look so tallowah this morning?"

I related all that happened with the lizard. Everything poured out of me like a waterfall. He looked at me with great affection as I recounted the entire story from the meeting under the guava tree to remembering the dream. He was very happy with me and laughed out loud, slapping me on the back gently and squeezing my shoulders. He had tears in his eyes. I felt so proud the way he treated me then. Tears welled up in my eyes, too. Bredda Man waited respectfully.

Then he gave me a piece of sugar cane and smiled as I peeled it with my teeth and chewed out all the juice and spat the pulp out onto the compost heap. A silence emerged from the depths of my being and I was still. I felt a great peace in simply being with my friend.

Bredda Man made some circe and pimento leaf tea. He offered me some, and I had to put honey in mine because it tasted so strong. He said, "Whenever it's cold, whoever drinks this won't get fever or anything that hurts their chest!" After we had finished, I washed out the cups.

I was thinking about the story again when Bredda Man spoke. "Knowledge is not always easy to express, but that is the job of Damah, when she remembers her husband and children. Is only when we believe say we body, imagination, heart and wisdom separate from each other, that we feel lonely." I felt a huge explosion of clarity when he said that.

My loneliness seemed to disappear as I realized my imagination existed for a reason and not just to scare me. I remembered the loneliness I felt when I wanted to share with my parents what I had learned, but could not. "Why don't more people care about this knowledge?" I asked, remembering the gut wrenching intuition that telling my family all of this would be a wasted effort.

Bredda Man looked serious and then he smiled. "That is the last part of the story, allowing ourselves to learn without fear from the deepest parts of ourselves. That is the knowledge of the seamless garment of the universe." He looked at me piercingly, and his look reminded me of the lizard's glare. I started to chuckle. He laughed, too. "The seamless garment of the universe" echoed through my being, and all I could do was chuckle!

Recalling my dream in clear detail, I became scared and lost all over again. But there was my brother snoring away beside me, and as I looked around the room I realized, slowly, breath by breath, I was safe and far away from the terrible helplessness of that memory. Then I remembered what Bredda Man had said about the lizard bringing me a great gift—the gift of remembering.

The Ananci story drifted back into my consciousness, weaving itself into a dreamlike mist. I was shocked by the sudden realization that I had just discovered the "curse" my imagination had buried in my heart. I remembered the story... I had tricked my imagination into paying attention to my problem for long enough that it remembered the cause buried in my past. Like Damah learning to repeat the names of the children over and over till she remembered, I had held the intention to remember in my body and heart for long enough to get back to the source of my fear. Then I realized: dreams are part of imagination. I had dreamed the next part of the story.

Now I had made it to the river and thrown Damah in. The curse had been lifted. I felt the power of life in me again starting to move and flow without fear.

I marveled at the process Bredda Man had orchestrated to help me understand the way my being worked, not as separate parts but as a whole. In applying the meaning of mastery to the entire circle of life I had initiated the work of remembering my wholeness from within. My own being was sending me the answers that connected the separate pieces of my heart.

I had feared the message the lizard brought me as a "bad" thing. But now I realized for the first time, the lizard didn't intend to hurt me. It was my not being able to express myself that was the problem. Then I remembered, "dumb beast" again. My fright in the experience with the lizard many years before was aggravated by the impotence I felt in being unable to com-

Bredda Man spoke again. "Come," he said, "let us go and hunt some birds together!"

I was surprised that Bredda Man would ask me to go hunting with him. I reminded him of my "problem" with slingshots and that I had not felt drawn to hunt anymore. But his confidence and warmth easily overcame my doubts and fears. I was beginning to feel excited as I followed him up the dirt bank of the gully into the bush.

Bredda Man moved like a snake, gliding around every bush and tree, as if he was dancing in a loving way with each of them as his partner. On the other hand, I smashed and pushed my way clumsily through the wilderness with increasing frustration. Bredda Man grimaced and winced each time I crashed through another bush or stomped on another twig. I was relieved when he suggested we return to the road. I knew he was being kind, by not telling me my noise was unbearable. But my recent excitement and joy disappeared quickly into a feeling of total failure once again.

I had never noticed before how insensitive I was. I didn't have anything to measure my clumsiness against when I was alone. But as we had moved through the bush together, I clearly saw and felt my own uneasiness and self-consciousness compared to Bredda Man's way of moving and being in nature.

I realized Bredda Man was moving from a different place than I was. He was moving from a loving, quiet and peaceful place in his heart, while I moved from an agitated, isolated place that made me fight against whatever I touched. Bredda Man moved effortlessly through the bush while I fought and struggled as if I were in a battle.

Hunting birds was not merely about a physically effort, it was about training the mind and heart to be still. It had to do with listening and being able to differentiate between one thought and another. It had to do with organizing and discriminating. My thoughts were all jumbled up. The bush was a reflection of how I moved through my own inner world.

Everything I came into contact with, it seemed, was attacking me…was an affront, an obstacle to my mastery! While Bredda Man moved as if everything he touched was caressing him or dancing with him. I thought, because I understood mastery now in a deeper way, I would be over my difficulties. The truth was, understanding only opened the door to the changes that needed to take place in my habits. Before I understood what mastery really meant, I thought I didn't have to do anything. Life was easy. All of a sudden my understanding was merely the pitiful first step in a marathon journey. Now I had a lot of work to do!

Back at the road Bredda Man said comfortingly, "Let's make a new slingshot for you before we go hunting again."

I was glad he still wanted to spend time with me. I started to relax about the mountain of work that loomed up ahead of me.

Bredda Man told me to go home and get some rubber and shoe tongue leather while he searched out the right crooks for us. I found some truck tire inner tubes in the garage that old Maas Harvey had given me for my slingshots and some old leather shoes. I cut enough rubber for twenty slingshots and set off back to Bredda Man.

By the time I got back to Bredda Man, he had cut and shaved two beautiful crooks of guava wood. He looked at the rubber and smiled. He pulled it and snapped it. It was very sharp and snappy. "That's good rubber! Nowadays everywhere you look, you can only find 'draw an stop' rubber… and that has no snap at all in it!"

Bredda Man said I should watch carefully how he made his slingshot, and then copy him.

The first thing I noticed was how attentively Bredda Man worked. His hands treated the wood and rubber as if they were his friends. I watched the miracle of his engineering take place before my eyes. His slingshot was beautiful. Then I set about trying to reproduce his movements.

I was very nervous working under his watchful eye. I sweated profusely. When I put the final touches on my slingshot and laid it next to his, mine looked like a junkyard car compared to a Cadillac!

We tested the slingshots. I was awed by the accuracy and power of the one Bredda Man had made. But as for mine, it was the embarrassing walk in the bush all over again. He smiled and teased me. "The only thing you going to do with that, is knock down the old and sick birds." He made a gesture suggesting that my slingshot would serve me best as a club. We laughed together, and I was relieved a bit of my embarrassment by his joking.

Bredda Man remade my slingshot for me. As I watched again, I saw how I had missed certain key points in the building process, the most significant being a profound stillness that was the source of his every movement.

As we put the finishing touches on the slingshots, the Sun was drawing high in the morning sky. I wanted to ask Bredda Man about walking in the woods together, and why I felt so uncomfortably aware of my own agitation behind the face of my clumsiness. I dreaded going back into the woods again.

I was tense. I waited, thinking about the way to ask the question so I would not sound stupid. Finally, I could not bring myself to ask him. As soon as I decided to put off what I wanted to ask, he stood up and stretched. He yawned and sighed. I was aware that his reaction coincided just so with my cowardice.

Then, as if to shatter any illusions of security in my own secret world, he said with a big grin on his face, "We better meet again soon, in case you have something to ask bout."

At first I was barely able to move or breathe. I felt as if I had been caught red-handed. I must have actually turned red, because Bredda Man chuckled and teased me.

"A what happen… Sun too hot this time a day?" He said, laughing softly.

His laughter put me more at ease again. I was glad he would give me another chance to ask my question. I made a gift of the remaining rubber to Bredda Man. He cut it into neat strips and gave me back some to keep.

I watched Bredda Man walk away. The Sun was winking at me over his shoulder as he disappeared over the ridge of the hill. Then I turned and started slowly home.

I felt as if I was no longer alone in the world. Why had I felt alone for all those years? "Dumb beast…dumb beast!" kept going through my head. I knew that my imagination could understand and make sense of the teaching stories. That was my self-assigned task…to feel that what I knew was coming out of the dark room. It gave me a sense of freedom.

As I reached the long winding driveway to our home, my mom was just driving up. I jumped on the bumper of the car and held onto the roof rack and she took off slowly up the road. After being a complete clumsy oaf in the forest I was finally able to have some fun.

When we got to the house, I jumped off the bumper and helped carry the groceries inside. I felt really happy and peaceful. I gazed out with a tremendous love to the mountains around our home. The little spark of joy I felt deep inside me shouted out loud, "Thank you!" to all of nature.

I heard her say quietly, "I feel like that, too, sometimes."

I did not need to ask her what she meant. She smiled, and I felt a great power smiling upon us and holding us in the grace of that moment.

# 3

# Learning to Listen

THE NEXT TIME I saw Bredda Man he was at the mall on Constant Spring Road. His brown skin glistened in the hot afternoon sunlight. He had several of his carvings with him, neatly wrapped up with newspaper in a crocus bag and packed into a cardboard box.

He stood beside a brightly painted pushcart, chatting with the vendor who was selling roasted cashew nuts and jelly coconuts, "Jah Merciful Sweet Water."

Behind the wagon, a fire blazed under a small mahogany tree, blackening the zinc that covered two charred concrete blocks. Roasting on the makeshift grill, the cashew nut husks turned dark as the oil spit and fizzled on the open flames.

I looked longingly at some of the fresh juicy yellow fruit still on the cashews in an open crocus bag next to the fire. The vendor glanced at Bredda Man and then smiled at me. "I don't like to eat the fruit off the cashews … go on and eat them, maan … just leave the nuts for the fire."

I was more than happy to help the vendor prepare the nuts for roasting by eating the fruits attached to the shiny grey nut husks. Cashew nut juice tastes like a mixture of light oil, delicate pepper, and orange juice. The pulp is hard to swallow because it leaves your mouth so dry that you tend to choke at first. Cashew fruit is not to everyone's taste, but it is definitely to mine! I had eaten about ten of the cashew fruits before I even slowed down.

"Whoaa, that will put lead in the pencil, maan!" Said the old man, laughing.

After I put the dry flesh from the fruits into a big oil drum that was used for the coconut husks, I gathered the nuts together on the zinc and cleaned them and placed the fruit on the grass, ready for when he needed them.

The old man prepared a coconut and handed it to me. He wouldn't take any money from Bredda Man for the coconut. He smiled contentedly and nodded and smiled again, saying, "My little bredda work for him food."

I was proud to feel that in the old man's eyes I had earned the gift of the coconut.

It was a busy Saturday market day. The green and grey JOS (Jamaica Omnibus Service) buses were bringing vendors who had missed the early service. They would have to struggle now to find a spot in the market or share a space with a friend.

My dad called the JOS "the Jamaican Obituary Service." And anyone who has ridden in a JOS bus will understand this joke, knowing that it is a scary, near-death experience to ride a Jamaican bus through the countryside.

I looked around at the colors of the foods on display. Breadfruit, green banana, mangos, guinneps, oatie eatie apples, soursop, sweetsop, susumba, peas, beans, pumpkin, cassava, yam, ackee, plantain, bissy, chainy root, ginger, gungu peas, dry pimento, tamarind, sweets of all types and colors, spices, herbal remedies, and tonics.

Chickens with their legs tied up lay calmly in rows, while numerous goats and pigs stood side by side foraging in the concrete pens between the rows of market stalls. People argued and made deals in the hustle and bustle.

The vendor smiled at me and said kindly, "Cokenut water is the only one go straight to the heart. Yes, maan, it go straight to the heart." A man nearby added, "You never hear about those soldier boys overseas … they use the cokenut water for blood transfusions when they get wounded! Yes, maan." Then another blurted out, "What are you saying! Gwaaay…. Maan, you blouw wow…. What are you saying about them using jelly cokenut for blood."

An old woman selling vegetables—ackee and breadfruit, yam and sweet potato—joined in. "Who tells you say cokenut water can't be used for blood … they take it to feed animals when their mothers don't have milk… what makes you old ignorant men, fool fool so!" She sucked her teeth and turned, smiling sweetly in Bredda Man's direction.

Bredda Man chuckled as the old men laughed at themselves, and the old woman blushed. Bredda Man said to the old woman, "Miss Rachel tell me something, how are your children going on?"

The mood changed and everyone was respectfully quiet.

Miss Rachel looked sad and sucked her teeth again, "Bwaaay! Bredda Man it's a long time now since I heard from my boy… he is growing up too fast and I can't help him at all. He acts as if he is a big man. He a carries a rachet knife and kerchief in his trouser pocket now…ahoah! He likes to go on about he is a rude boy!" She shook her head sadly.

Bredda Man put his hand on her shoulders. He said, "Don't worry Miss Rachel, we are going to talk to the boy and see if he will come back to help you again!"

The old men whispered in the background. Miss Rachel looked up at Bredda Man and smiled, her big soft eyes almost welling up with tears. "Thank you, Bredda Man…Gahd bless you, Bredda Man, Gahd Bless you!" She held his hand and kissed it warmly.

When Bredda Man said he would talk to the boy, it was serious business. If an elder spoke to someone the whole town would know what was going on.

Suddenly, all in a rush, a young mixed-blood boy came charging up on his bike with his little brother perched on the handlebars. He asked anxiously if anyone had seen their dog.

Bredda Man listened and looked around, as if he was sensing something, and then he said reassuringly to the boys, "Your bredda is not lost…it's you that is lost."

The boys looked confused and nervous. Something in the way Bredda Man had said it, made them realize he was right, but that did not stop them from feeling agitated and defensive. They were about to dash off, but Bredda Man asked them if they wanted some jelly coconuts. He watched calmly as the boys eyed the delicious coconuts. Then he whispered something to the vendor and he sat down on the grass. He took out a red cloth bundle from his bag and unwrapped a small pipe. The bowl was made of red stone inlaid with four circles of silver. A wooden stem fit inside the red stone bowl.

When he took out the pipe the elders sitting nearby became very quiet. There was an air of reverence. Bredda Man lit the pipe and took a few puffs. He blew the smoke toward Miss Rachel and the elders, and then toward the boys. Then he extinguished the pipe and placed it carefully back in his bag.

The vendor searched around in his street cart for some coconuts. He examined one and then another while the sweaty, thirsty boys looked on. Each time we thought he was about to chop one, he would put it back and say, "No sir… that one's not sweet enough for my little pardy!" Finally he found one and started to cut it. I have never seen a coconut so carefully cleaned and cut before. The vendor cleaned and scraped every dust particle off the coconut before handing it over to the bigger boy. While the smaller boy jealously watched his brother down the coconut juice, the old man started the same painfully slow, comedic drama all over again.

Just then a big white wolf dog came running up, wagging its tail. The dog was obviously overjoyed to see the boys, but they were too busy watching the vendor cleaning their coconuts. The dog made his way quietly, crawling on his belly, over to where Bredda Man sat and silently and respectfully settled in front of him. When Bredda Man nodded to the vendor, he suddenly stopped looking for coconuts and grabbed the first one he laid his hands on. In a tenth of the time it took him to clean and prepare the first one, the second one was done.

The little brother was looking very suspiciously at the shabby coconut handed to him. He had obviously expected the same pomp and ceremony associated with his big brother's coconut.

Bredda Man laughed and teased him, "We were making a joke with you, my little bredda... if we never kept you here, your bredda dog couldn't find you. Your bredda dog was trying to find you but you were moving around too fast. That's why we kept you in one place long enough for him to find you."

The big brother suddenly noticed his dog sitting with Bredda Man like a king on his throne. When he got over the shock of his dog finding *him*, he playfully stroked the dog and attached a lead to the dog's collar.

Unmoved by what Bredda Man said. The younger brother simply looked, truly dismayed, at his coconut. He put it down on the cart and sulked, crossing his arms stiffly, refusing to move. His older brother teased him by laughing and sucking his teeth. The elders chuckled and whispered mischief at the young boy's stubborn antics.

Feeling sorry for him, the kind vendor smiled and shook his head. He patiently cleaned and cut the young boy's coconut, making it look even more ceremonial than he had done before. Then and only then, savoring both the juice and the drama, would the little brother drink his jelly coconut.

The older brother got on his bike, obviously annoyed his younger brother had been successful. Finally, they rode off together, arguing about whose coconut had been nicer, with all of us laughing hysterically at their display of sibling rivalry.

Bredda Man paid for the boys' coconuts and gave the vendor a tip for mine. We all laughed and joked about that little boy's contented face.

I was curious to know how Bredda Man knew the dog was looking for the boys. "Bredda Man, how did you know the dog would find them if they stayed in one place for long enough?"

Bredda Man smiled and replied, "I knew from watching them two boys. They love the dog…. and dogs always know when they friends are upset. The dog will always find those boys because they are like her own children to her."

What he said made sense but I would never have thought of any of that myself.

When we were ready to leave the market, we set off up Stony Hill Road together. Many people tooted their horns to Bredda Man as we walked. Some stopped to ask if we wanted a lift. Bredda Man chatted for a few seconds and blessed them with his big-hearted smile, and they drove off feeling better. Bredda Man gave one driver his box of carvings and asked him to drop it off at the gas station at the big bend in the road.

Halfway up the hill, we met an old man with old car tires strapped to his feet for shoes. He raised his head to nod respect for Bredda Man. Like many old country people he looked about fifty years old, but he could have been well into his eighties, and still strong and tallowah! He wore his self-made, car tire shoes proudly.

I lowered my eyes because he was an elder, and he had acknowledged me with a very subtle glance. Bredda Man put his hand on my shoulder. I respectfully looked away. When I looked up again, I thought I saw the old man smile as he strode past us toward the market, his big car tire shoes flapping on the tarmac. I felt the old man's presence long after he passed us. Bredda Man and I walked on in silence, honoring that old man's being, feeling his impression in our hearts till it faded away in the silence.

After we had walked on for some distance, Bredda Man teased me, "When you going to make shoes for me… little bredda?"

I laughed and said, "As soon as I find two old car tires."

When we arrived at the gas station, the box of carvings was sitting neatly inside the front door of the garage office. The young attendant nodded respectfully as Bredda Man picked up the carvings.

We sat down on the grass by the side of the path up to the Stony Hill Hotel. "Bredda Man, how can I learn to walk like you in the bush without making any noise?" I asked quietly and sighed, relieved that I had finally managed to ask for something I cared about.

Bredda Man looked at me, relieved, too. My question seemed to give him great pleasure. He said, "I am glad you're listening to your heart now. That is the start of our journey, little bredda…. when we start to listen to our heart … that is the start of our learning."

He began to sort through the carvings, taking great care to organize them so he could carry them on his head the rest of the way up the steep hill.

I thought he had forgotten about my question, but then he looked at me and smiled. "Go into the bush and sit down until you can hear the birds walking!"

I laughed, believing he was teasing me. I half expected him to squint up his eyes and laugh again, but he looked at me patiently and seriously until I realized he was not joking.

I felt stupid again, but he smiled gently to reassure me. He was clear about what was required, and if I wanted to learn, it was a simple choice—JUST DO IT. I had my answer. I promised myself I would learn to listen.

Bredda Man picked up his carvings and started the long walk up to the top of the hill.

The next day I set out for the bush. I walked a long while, venturing into an area I had never been before. I sat down on the edge of the forest thicket where the earth was red. The Sun beat down on the lush green canopy above me.

The first thing I saw was some ant lion's traps, little cone shaped dunes into which bugs fall for the ant lions to grab and devour. For a while, I watched the red ants scurrying around picking up pieces of the forest to take to their home. Then I watched the john chewits and auntie katies coming to feed on the paw paw trees.

I was too anxious to sit still for more than a minute or two, so I got up and paced around, throwing stones to pass the time, and generally feeling bored. I had a gnawing feeling I should be focusing on listening, but I was too caught up in resisting and struggling with my impatience, to be able to focus.

As the Sun set, I gave up, feeling even worse than before about my uneasiness and discomfort. I wanted to hide from everyone, especially Bredda Man. The next morning I wondered about trying again. "Why am I spending my summer holidays doing this," I asked myself. I could not exactly answer my question, but I realized then, I was not going to quit, and I never needed to ask that question again.

The second day was easier because I was more relaxed and peaceful. But I daydreamed most of the day, and when it came time to go home, I left hurriedly, feeling like I hadn't really tried to listen in the way Bredda Man had said.

The third day, my space was becoming very familiar and I settled in quickly, thinking that I should try a little harder. But, again, as my boredom and agitation got the better of me, I thought again about giving up.

I was afraid to listen for some reason. Whenever I tried to just listen, there always seemed to be an impulse to do something else. Then I dared myself to try to really listen.

Suddenly, I felt as if Bredda Man was standing there and at the same moment, I saw a big green iguana on a burnwood tree stretch out his heart flag and bob his head. I felt as if he was telling me to concentrate and try harder.

It was unnerving to look at the iguana's old man face. His eyes glared at me, compelling me to focus on the work at hand. Now I was backed into a corner. Really letting myself be present and receptive was a risk, and I was scared to take the risk.

The iguana glared at me again and bobbed his head assertively. I dared and double dared myself not to back down. I started to listen to one sound at a time. I chose the sound of a bird singing in the distance. I listened intently. As I listened, my breath smoothed out and I started to calm down.

I got distracted, but each time I went back to really focusing on listening to that one sound and then I felt calm. The difference was astonishing. It was as if I turned on a switch. A deep peace descended over me.

I started to feel the listening as a deeply tranquil sensation or posture in my body. Before I knew it, I was totally focused and relaxed, and the forest around me seemed like it was my home. There was nothing to do and nowhere to be, except where I was. All the anxiety of the previous days, was gone. I felt somehow the listening was a state where I was totally at peace with nature.

I decided to focus even deeper on my listening. I started to listen to the sounds in my own body. I listened to my heartbeat. Then I listened to the sounds and rhythms in different parts of my body. They seemed to echo the sounds of the birds and insects around me. I felt as if the creatures around me were voicing some mysterious force, each with their own unique sounds.

This listening opened a vast universe. Suddenly I was in a sea of sounds and vibrations that spread through the living forest. I felt an immense presence in that place as I listened. I was wide-awake, but it felt like I was dreaming.

I was drifting peacefully from one sound to another when something crashing through the underbrush called me abruptly back to my place. I started to focus on this sound as it came closer. My entire being contracted and my calm changed to a state of intense alertness. I got up very carefully and hid behind a big guinnep tree until I could get a glimpse of what was coming. I listened with every fiber of my being.

When it sounded as if the creature was directly in front of me, I cautiously ventured to look around the edge of the tree. I was totally shocked at what I saw. I stood up and strode out from behind my tree, staring in absolute amazement at a white winged dove! I couldn't believe that the huge racket I was listening to was the sound his feet made on the ground.

When I emerged suddenly from behind the tree, almost close enough to touch him, the terrified dove flew away in a desperate panic, leaving many of his downy chest feathers floating in the air behind him.

Watching him disappear over the last few trees along the horizon, I tried to regain my composure and calm my still wildly beating heart. I looked around. A few fluffy white feathers from the dove floated around in the bush. I caught one on my hand. As I felt its soft warm texture, I imagined I could feel the heart of the dove beating gently. I felt a deep tenderness toward the dove and I wished him well. I found myself apologizing to him for frightening him with my carelessness.

I suddenly realized I had completed my task. I felt differently about the forest now. Actually, it was myself that I felt differently about. I had experienced myself as a part of Creation and I had made a connection to an awareness that was without boundaries or time. I was able to feel and hear Creation with reverence for the first time.

I was not agitated or scared anymore. I was no longer trapped in the swarming buzz of my thoughts and internal dialogue. I had given my hungry wisdom the ripe, juicy fruit of my agitation and impatience. My peace had been awakened because of the nourishment I gave it, and now I was awake in the peaceful knowing of my heart.

This time I did not hurry to leave the forest. I walked home slowly, enjoying the new sensitivity I had discovered. I wanted to know everything intimately. I touched leaves and flowers with a tender reverence and felt their receptivity. Now there was no carelessness or impatience in our meeting. It seemed as if we knew we were each part of a timeless oneness. In this oneness the plants, the trees, the animals, all of nature saw I was open to being present and echoed the peace I felt.

# 4

# Burning Bridges

MY CLASS consisted of twenty children from many different backgrounds and races. We were various combinations of Chinese, Indian, African, and Europeans. That's how it is with Jamaican families, all mixed up, just like our class. On the coat of arms in the school assembly hall, hidden behind the statue of the Virgin Mary, the motto under the images of two Arawak indians and an alligator announced, "Out of Many, One People."

It was a still, hot day. We had finished playing our usual round of lunchtime games. A soda bottle from the vending machine in the playground had exploded on a picnic table in the heat of the Sun. We sat around it watching a thick white foam ooze through the cracked glass like a dying worm writhing in the Sun. The school bell clanged loudly, calling us back to our lessons.

Sister Corilla's was the first lesson after lunchtime. Her classroom was tucked beneath a huge poincianna tree on the ground floor of the convent school Immaculate Conception, which stood proudly beside the Constant Spring Golf Course.

If anyone represented the Catholic church in my life, it was Sister Corilla. She was an awesome figure—a giant in my eyes—even though she walked with a cane.

We were getting another hellfire and brimstone lecture. I was wondering about being terrorized by a God who needed someone like Sister Corilla to prove that having sex made people impure and in need of a stiff preaching to bring them back into the fold. This philosophy always seemed out of place in Jamaica where there were so many large families with mixed skin colors that showed otherwise. Everyone, it seemed, took this part of the rules with a pinch of salt … maybe even a handful. And most of Sister Corilla's other rules didn't make sense to us either. So we just simplified them to make it easier for ourselves. Being scared of her meant being good and not being scared of her meant being bad. That worked for most of the time.

Sister Corilla seemed very confident and secure in her religious beliefs. But I felt uncomfortable around her and I couldn't understand why. Her awe-inspiring, fearsome lectures—like the cold water I was told would be poured over me if I didn't get up for church service on Sunday morning—did nothing to relieve my doubts about integrity in that institution.

She was ranting on, in her strange, hollow voice, speaking with vehemence, her eyes glaring with fanatical fervor. "When you have Jesus as your Savior, you are fearless to face any problem in life."

Almost as soon as those words left her mouth, a chaotic ruckus broke out that sounded like the devil himself was dragging mountains down the hallway outside our classroom. We all froze in our seats.

In a flash, and without any thought for us, Sister Corilla made her escape—her black habit flapping in the wind behind her as she disappeared through the open classroom window——just as a real-life dairy cow appeared in the concrete hallway. It ambled clumsily down the hallway, dragging its long, heavy, clanking chain, and stuck its head through the classroom door as if to say, "Oops ... sorry, I made a wrong turn!" God, it seems, has a wicked sense of humor.

My first reaction was to shout out loud, "Halleluyah! The Lord has sent a replacement!"

The class nervously exploded into hysterical laughter.

So the truth had been revealed about this hypocritical preacher. It was pathetic to me that she had been such a coward and had left us all in harm's way.

I realized, then, that I had been mentally and emotionally shoring up the discomfort I felt around Sister Corilla, as well as all the other church people I knew who were at odds with life. I had been trying desperately to tell myself these pillars of the community were really important and caring people. In the midst of all this commotion, I suddenly felt myself let go of the great myth of Sister Corilla and the entire church system. I was free!

Back in the classroom, I could see that many of the children were afraid of this lumbering, confused creature. Since I had spent many summers on a dairy farm I knew enough to realize that if I could get hold of the chain in the cow's nose ring, then she would feel safe again. With the help of one of the other boys, I managed to get hold of her and calm her. As we were taking her outside, the worried herdsman was fast approaching. He had chased off the stray dogs that had frightened his herd and was intent on rescuing the last of his cows. His big, rolled down rubber boots flopped around as he came stomping toward us with his long beard and wild hair and eyes, like some ancient old prophet.

Sister Corilla stood stiffly in the dusty playground, brushing away the hundreds of tiny poincianna's leaves that clung to her habit. But her hands were covered with dust, and soon she had handprints of dust, as well as the poincianna leaves, smeared all over her habit. She glared at me. But now, unwaveringly, I could look her in the eyes.

In an attempt to regain some measure of her power, Sister Corilla tried to intimidate the herdsman by calling him an ignorant country man. But that didn't faze the mixed-blood herdsman, With a knowing look, he completely dismissed her.

When he saw the two of us keeping his cow safely under the huge canopy of the poincianna, he came over to us and took hold of the chain. He gently shook our hands, thanking us with a big grin.

Time stopped when the old herdsman took my hand. We looked at each other and I felt I knew who he was. His deep, warm smile reassured me and challenged me to trust my sense of knowing. I had thought about being loyal to Sister Corilla and defend her "dignity" by telling him off, but then I looked in his eyes and saw the truth. I watched my well-mannered illusions go down in the flames of his warm-hearted smile.

The herdsman turned and strode away. We stood watching in amusement at Sister Corilla hurrying after him, shouting indignantly.

Then, at the same moment, both of us realized that we were witnessing a miracle. As we stood watching her pursue that old herdsman—there was Sister Corilla's cane laying in the dust at our feet.

We looked at each other wide-eyed—Sister Corilla had been healed! In awe, I picked up the cane and held it out to her when she returned. As soon as she saw me with her cane, Sister Corilla suddenly remembered she had a bad hip. She grabbed the cane and pushed roughly past us toward the classroom, limping painfully, as ever before.

Her limp was an act! Marching back into the classroom behind her, we began to imitate her limping. She turned around quickly, sensing we were up to mischief. But we were even quicker. We stopped and looked off into the distance, to watch the herdsman as he disappeared around the corner and off the convent land.

I felt that something in me had shifted on a deeply spiritual level. I had been shown something very powerful about bullies and empire builders. I saw that the person I had held up as a hero was just a lonely, frightened human being. Sister Corilla could not accept herself in that vulnerable way, and she could not allow others to see her that way either. She had to manipulate everyone to feel sorry for her, including herself, by making up a more acceptable weakness.

Sister Corilla now sat in the classroom, feeling as if she had been redeemed. She looked at the two of us for confirmation. My friend and I returned, disinterested, to our places. The other children were huddled over their desks, afraid to show they had seen what happened outside. But I knew that we had all seen the truth that day about Sister Corilla.

Sister Corilla, I thought, had to see her openness as a weakness. She did not really want relationship.... she used her cane to trick herself into believing her vulnerability was a limp. She could never relax and be a true friend because she actually believed her own lie. Her ultimate failure was one of trust—the trust that enables people who truly know that God exists to share themselves with others.

Sister Corilla at first tried to draw me back into the fold gently. But neither her sermons nor her praise meant anything to me anymore. When praise did not work, she started beating me to renew my "spiritual fervor" and to validate her need for asserting power and authority. The more she tried to get me to confirm her beliefs, the less I responded. I felt her sense of futility when she saw that everything she did to intimidate me simply confirmed my own knowing.

Sister Corilla's heart, it seemed, was greatly troubled by her actions in the cow incident. But it seemed wrong that because of God's little trick, I was demonized to justify her feelings of unworthiness and cowardice.

God, however, was not finished with me. Because I had thought it was only Sister Corilla who needed a lesson, it was soon my turn for God to play a trick on.

I had been chosen to carry a tray of flowers from statue to statue in the May procession on a trail around the school. I did this reluctantly because I was still feeling angry and rebellious. As I approached the statue of a saint surrounded by animals, a beam of light descend from the sky and surrounded me. I was totally quieted by the reverent calm the light invoked in me.

The priest was trying to hurry me along, but I wanted to remain in the beam of light. Then I heard the word "trust!" The beam followed me as I walked around the rest of the trail until I finally realized it was there for me to learn something about a true religious experience. The feeling I had now was the same as I had experienced when I listened in the bush.

As I neared the group of priests, nuns and parents gathered at the end of the procession, the beam faded away. I felt tingly, high-as-a-kite and wide-awake. I realized no one else knew anything of what I had seen. I started to get an idea that the true religious experience that so many people yearned for at church was not controlled by those who wear robes and imposed harsh rules. Now I could see a deeper level to religion. This level was free and available to everyone—and to every spiritual organization.

I was sorry that I couldn't stay in that beautiful light but I took comfort in the thought of seeing Bredda Man again soon and the renewed possibility for trust that his teachings brought me.

Later on I found out the statue was Saint Francis, and I studied about his life and thought. St. Francis reminded me of Bredda Man.

I stood by the gully Bredda Man used as a shortcut, looking hopefully up and down the steep gorge. Soon I saw him walking toward me smiling. He was going up into the mountains to collect some herbal medicines, and I was invited to come with him.

As we left the dirt tracks and entered the bush I felt Bredda Man listening to me and sensing me behind him. I was aware of the distance between us like a thick atmosphere. I moved through the bush in reverence, listening and feeling that I was plugged into the living presence of the wilderness. I drew the living cloak of green and blue around me and followed my guide.

After about twenty minutes we stopped and Bredda Man turned to me with a proud smile, "Tell me what happen when you sat in the bush by your self."

"I heard the dove walking."

Bredda Man watched me intently, waiting for something more to be said.

"I was listening to the bird and cricket noises, too, and I felt it in my body like an echo of something bigger than all of us."

Bredda Man smiled a huge smile and nodded his head, and we continued on our way. We stopped once to pick some ripe rose apples. Bredda Man popped the crisp, delicate skin open so I could smell the sweet fragrance that gives its name to the yellow fruit.

When we arrived at a place where village farmers had cleared the trees and bush, Bredda Man stopped to observe a swarm of butterflies hovering above the grassy clearing. We sat down and watched as they drifted off. Then, one by one, different wild birds landed on the same spot and rested for a minute before going on their way.

After a few minutes we walked over to the spot and Bredda Man looked around to orientate himself. He pulled out some green bush and cornmeal from his pack, and spread it in a circle around the spot, which was nothing more than a green clump of wild flowers and grasses. He showed me that the Earth was cool there, and that it meant water was welling up underneath. Then we moved on again, following trails I had never been on before.

In the years to come I would accompany Bredda Man many times when he went to collect herbs in the bush to use as medicine. This time he picked from several different plants —susumba, pea, circe, pimento, and kola— and also from some wild fruit trees.

Whenever we approached a tree or bush to harvest, Bredda Man surveyed it carefully. He offered his prayers to each tree or bush before he took anything. "Bredda Bissy, I come to take a little piece of you family to use to help my people. I thank you to give me your medicine with so much love and peace." Then he would cut or pluck gently from a certain area of the plant or tree. He always looked first for the new shoots that would grow over or block a pathway. Then he helped the tree or plant by removing them.

He also helped the tree by removing its dead limbs and said this was a way to "train'" the tree to enjoy his visits and remember him with fondness. Sometimes he sang a song for the tree or left some strands of his hair tied like a little present to make the tree feel good.

After we had picked almost a whole crocus bag full of medicines, fruits and herbs, we sat down to talk.

"You know what they say the medicine of the lizard is?" He asked me, looking at me seriously. I shook my head.

"They say it's to heal burns on anybody's skin. They say the lizard medicine works also to heal burns inside, too… it's to hold onto fire without getting burned. That is the medicine of awakening." I was shaken by what he said.

"Do I have to do that?" I asked looking worried.

He smiled. "If the lizard gives you their gift it's between you both how you use it."

I sat still for a while, worrying about finding out if I could heal people's burns and not get burned by fire. The thought seemed too much for me to handle. It suddenly occurred to me that I did not really know what he meant. "How do I know if the lizard wants me to have their gift?" I asked.

"The gifts from nature always have two sides, first there is a wounding and then they become open to you. It's they who pick you. When they are ready and know you are ready, they will come to you and show you they are open to you. If they come to you in a dream that is the small gift. If they come in the natural world…then that is the most powerful gift.

"When you see they open to you.… If you lick their belly three times … that means you are willing to take the gift from them and you are their bredda ever afterwards. If you kill lizards after that time you will suffer great illness. Nor must you eat their meat nor any of their family neither, like snake nor eel. That means you complete the healing with their medicine. Then is up to you when and how you decide to use it. Moses was initiated by the snake in the same way."

Bredda Man looked at me and smiled. He saw my anxiety in my wrinkled-up face for how much of a responsibility I thought the lizard's gift would be.

He went on. "Lizard have one bredda, Maas Bedford, I know about, that has the gift. People come to see him when they family gets a burn and the doctors can't help. One time a boy got burned so bad on his face, his family said he would die because the burns got infected and the doctor couldn't do anything at all."

I was intrigued, "What did the lizard man do? "

Bredda Man winced a little bit, as he chewed slowly on a pimento leaf. "Well, he drank off half a bottle of Appleton and then he licked the burn off the boy's face with his tongue."

The thought of licking infected flesh made me dizzy.

Bredda Man continued, "the boy got better, sure as the Sun must shine. Nobody could tell he ever got burned. But not everyone of the lizard man heals in the same way."

I was becoming more and more horrified by the thought of being a lizard man.

Bredda Man laughed, teasingly, and said, "They might never come to you, so don't fret yourself!"

I felt relieved and scared at the same time. I wasn't sure it was a good idea to have made friends with the lizard after all.

We left the bush and made our way back to the gully. As we parted, Bredda Man gave me some pimento leaf to take for my mom to use as seasoning. I went home in solemn silence. I felt like I had gotten myself into something I could not see any way out of. I could not hate lizards any more, but I wasn't sure I wanted to love them that much either.

Every time I saw a lizard after that, I remembered Maas Bedford licking the burned, infected face. I shuddered and ran away as fast as I could, just in case one decided to give me its gift. The lizard's gift was not something I was ready for. But I couldn't forget it either.

I thought about the deeper part of the lizard's gift, healing inner wounds. I thought about what burns of a subtle nature would be. Bredda Man had said emotional power was fire. I thought if I accepted the lizard's gift I would be able to heal emotional wounds in myself and others. Then, I remembered the way I had found meaning in the Ananci story and how it connected to my own Life. I thought maybe I could heal people by helping them to use meaning in a whole-hearted way. After I thought about this I felt a whole lot better and I was not so afraid about the lizard's gift any more.

# 5

# Accepting the Lizard's Gift

IT WAS A SATURDAY afternoon. My parents were at Caymanas race track for the day, where one of my father's horses was racing. My brother Buck and I were out playing a game of cricket with friends in a field over by the big storm gully. We had found a couple of beat-up, cork-and-tar balls and cut out bats with a machete from some old pieces of fence post. The boundaries were set at the edge of the dirt field so if the ball rolled into the bush it scored a four, and if it flew into the bushes, it was a six.

My spin bowling was improving a lot. I could bowl a number of different spin pitches. The "leg-break" throw veered away from the wicket and the "off-break" throw turned first into and then away from the wicket upon bouncing. The "googly" was a medium-paced spinner. It hit the ground and stayed low. And then there was the "Yorkie," which didn't bounce at all. It was aimed directly at the wicket, but lobbed so that it dropped out of the sky right over the batsman.

With spin pitches the batsman couldn't tell which way the ball was going to turn, or how sharply, once it bounced. This usually forced the batsman into sudden reactions and errors in judgement. He could either risk coming toward the ball and hitting it just before it bounced or trying to hit it close after the bounce to minimize the angle of the spin. But misjudging the sudden turn after the bounce meant a desperate swipe, which usually ended up sending the ball high in the air and made it an easy catch.

My cousin Lorry had been skillfully managing my spins with his "No!" style by stepping forward and squashing the spin before the angle could deceive him. Then, just when I felt I was bowling to the length of his step, he hit me for six.

The ball flew deep into the bushes, and we had to stop the game for almost twenty minutes to look for it. When we got back to the game, I still was determined to get my cousin out. I bowled him a short leg-break, and as he stepped into it, it spun off his bat into the air. I was ready and dove for it... straight into a macka (thorn) bush. Afterward, I braved the wicket like a wounded soldier, proud that my clever but painful strategy had worked.

When we got home, Alec, one of my dad's stable hands, had cooked up some ackee and salt fish dasheen for lunch. We traded his for the curry mincemeat and rice that CeCe had made for us. We both thought it was a good trade.

We had hardly finished eating when CeCe started pushing us to have an afternoon nap because she wanted to go out with a friend. I was tired and bruised after playing cricket, so I was happy to lie down.

CeCe was moody from the rum she had been drinking all morning while we had been out playing. She staggered into the room, irritated that we were still awake, and started to slur her words, as she always did when she was drunk. When we giggled, she sobered up. She came and stood over me like a menacing guard dog and said in a threatening voice, "Go to sleep, child! You want me to give you two good hits in your Rass!"

I lay very still and waited a while. I opened my eyes to see if she was still there. She was! ... sure that I would purposely defy her. She grabbed her bamboo switch and started hitting me hard. "A who tell you say I am joking!" Whack! "You think say you're bad!" Whack! "You think say you can go on bad and rule me... nuh!" Whack! At first I tried to protect myself, but that only incited her to hit me harder and faster.

When I looked into her eyes, they were hollow and dead. I saw right into her soul. Her spirit was defeated, and she was lost in a sea of meaningless rage. Then, behind my fear, I saw the disgust I felt for her, and I knew that my fear of her had always been my way of trying not to show how much revulsion I felt for her.

CeCe flicked the bamboo so that it bent far back, and then whipped it into my back. Those blows stung even more than the heavy slaps. I decided to lie still and just let her hit me. If I pretended to be asleep, she would eventually stop. I took a last glance at my brother, his eyes wide in silent panic, as he watched me hide my spirit away.

CeCe kept hitting, but I didn't feel the switch anymore as it slapped and stung into my back and legs. I remember falling asleep with her standing over me and hitting me sporadically. I had moved into a space that she could not reach. I would return when she was gone.

When I woke up it was dark outside. I had shut down for longer than I thought. I looked in the mirror at the crisscrossed red marks my legs and back. There were scratches from the macka bush, too. All in all it was not that bad, I thought. I was unconcerned.

But when I sat down on the bed, the emotions I had put aside started to emerge. The sudden flood of emotion sent shudders through my body. I sobbed loudly. My brother came over and gently touched the marks.

Suddenly, we both had the same idea together. We found an old pen knife and retrieved CeCe's bamboo switch from behind the armchair. I cut into the cane. Each time I cut, I spoke as she did when she had hit me. "So you think say you bad!" Slice! "This cane here, when you hit me next, your will is going to shatter like this stick!" Slice!

We laughed as we made sure every joint on the stick was sliced through to the hollow core on one side or another. It would not break when it was swung, but the first thing it hit would shatter it into pieces. I realized I had spoken for my pain with a clear cool anger as I jointed the bamboo.

It felt powerful to use what Bredda Man had taught me. At first I felt nervous, guilty and mischievous. But the emotional heaviness that had burdened me, seemed to get lighter each time I sliced a joint on the cane and spoke out my pain. I felt I was taking my power back.

The next day CeCe had calmed down. It was Sunday, Church day, and she must have had a twinge of conscious because she couldn't look me in the eye. I decided to go hunting in the bush to get away from the house. My parents would drink with friends on Sunday afternoons and that wasn't much fun to be around either. It was times like these I liked the woods a lot more than home.

I took my slingshot and walked a long way into the bush before I started to become worried about getting lost. I sat down. I was alone in the forest and I was tired inside. I felt sad about the beating. I asked the woods, "Why?" and a gentle breeze blew across my face, tenderly reassuring me. I remembered the great beauty I had shared with Bredda Man, and I felt the same presence welcoming me. I sat with my hands on my knees and sobbed. I felt the spirit of the woods listen. I let go of the pain and the hurt. Then I wasn't sad any more. I felt clean again. I realized that only just now had I fully returned from the far away place where I went when I was being hit.

I was about to get up when I felt a weight shift on my leg. I thought my slingshot had fallen down onto my leg, but when I looked down, there sat the biggest iguana I have ever seen. He must have been there a while. He looked so peaceful, right at home, really. I was shocked because iguanas never usually come so close, much less perch on someone's leg.

I was scared to touch him, but I slowly moved my hand and lightly brushed his head. He blinked his eyes and then returned to his trancelike state. He seemed to have a smile on his face that was telling me he felt totally at peace and trusted me. Then I suddenly realized what was happening, This was it! The Lizard was here to give me his gift! I became extremely uncomfortable. I felt like running home. Instead, I sat quietly and thought about what Bredda Man had said to me about the gift. I wasn't sure, but something inside me said, if I do it, only the lizard and I need to know.

If I didn't tell anyone about the gift, nobody would ever ask me to lick their burn wounds. If I accepted the gift, maybe one day I would find another way to use it. Maybe there are burns of another kind that could be healed by this gift, too.

I reached down—the lizard was totally unconcerned —in fact, he almost seemed to be enjoying the whole drama. I took a deep breath and turned him upside down. I licked his belly three times. It was dry and scratchy and it tasted strange. Then I placed him back on my leg. He seemed quite content to sit there.

I kept swishing my tongue around in my mouth, tasting the strange flavor of the lizard. All at once, my body tingled as energy started to whirl and explode inside me like fireworks. The energy seemed to be circulating around my body in whirling vortices of light and heat, electricity and pressure. I became alarmed at how my whole body started to buzz. The thought crossed my mind that I had been poisoned. I wanted to get up and move around because of the agitation, but the iguana was resting so quietly I thought better of it. Then the energy seemed to calm down a bit so I closed my eyes and drifted off into a daydream about the cricket game.

When I opened my eyes, the lizard was gone. I looked everywhere for him, but it was as if he had never been there at all. I would have wondered if I had dreamed the whole thing, except that I still had the strange lizard taste in my mouth.

I never told anyone about that ritual. I never even told Bredda Man. I wasn't going to get pulled into licking people's festering wounds … No siree! I walked home through the forest that day feeling I had cleared my debt to the lizard. I felt I had been forgiven. I promised myself to use the lizard's gift to heal people's wounds somehow, as long as I did not have to lick burned skin. When I returned home it was almost dark. I didn't see CeCe around.

I went to the bathroom mirror to check my welts again, and to my astonishment, they were all gone. I knew I had been healed by accepting the gift of the lizard. This was another confirmation that I had not been dreaming. Now I was not afraid to face CeCe again. She could not hurt me anymore. I also felt, with a strong knowing, that she would never hit me again.

While I lay in bed that night, reading comic books by the light of my flashlight, I heard a car coming up the dirt road. I listened as the car pulled into the garage. Then there were loud drunken voices and the sound of thumping along the hallway.

Buck sat up, indignant. "Chu, maan, I'm tired of hearing fighting!" He shook his head sadly, realizing we had no idea what we could do to change our lives.

Since he was up I asked him to pick the grass lice off my back. He found about four ticks and we crushed them between our fingernails. I also had a splinter from the macka bush in my foot. When I finally managed to remove it. I held it in the tweezers and lit a match. "Go on back to where you come from!" I said intently, as I watched the splinter turn bright red and then disappear in the flame. With that splinter the weekend's poisoned memories were burned away, too.

All I could think about was the lizard's gift. It was good to be finally at peace with the lizards. Before I fell asleep I heard a croaker lizard call out in the darkness. I smiled, believing he was listening to my thoughts.

I woke up the next morning feeling bright again. I remembered that I had dreamed of the lizard. In my dream I watched him looking green and strong and healthy. Then he turned into a ball of light and rose into the air. When I looked up I saw a big John Crow gazing into my eyes as he circled around the sun. He flew right into the sun and disappeared into the blinding light. I knew the dream was a good sign.

# 6

# Meeting John Crow

SOME WEEKS LATER, Bredda Man and I were walking up in the mountains beside the river that runs above Constant Spring. I told Bredda Man about my dream. He smiled and nodded his head. I was never sure when he did that, whether he actually heard me or not, but I knew better than to ask. Bredda Man would answer when he was ready.

As we walked along, I asked him a question that I had been thinking about for a while, "Bredda Man, how can someone become powerful?"

Bredda man smiled and nodded his head again silently. He answered by asking me a question, "Is how the Sun feel on you back?"

I hadn't really paid attention to the Sun, but now I was aware of its warmth on my shoulders and back. Bredda Man stopped and turned round, and we started walking directly into the Sun. The Sun was now making me squint each time I looked up as we walked toward it.

"Tell me whether you believe say the Sun is powerful, more when the Sun is on your back or on your front?"

I thought for a while and realized it wasn't the fact that I noticed it that made the Sun powerful or not.

"It's powerful whether I feel it or not!" I said.

Bredda Man chuckled. "That's what most people believe makes something powerful, if they can remember it or not. Most people believe say whatever can wake them from sleep to remember something is what makes it powerful... but it's just like the Sun always shining and we do not remember it.

"Some people, even when we turn round, only think we feel better, when we walk toward the Sun. We don't even know the sunlight has anything to do with us feeling good, We only know about the direction we walk in."

I was still wondering how this related to my original question. I knew everything Bredda Man said related to the questions I asked. And I knew if I thought about it for a while the answer would get clearer to me. That's what I did. I started to get a sense of what he meant as I mulled it over.

"So it's not what we believe that makes something powerful, but knowing it doesn't matter whether we believe it or not, and yet still it is real, that makes it powerful? If we thought the Sun would not rise if we did not believe in it...we wouldn't know it as powerful!"

Bredda Man stopped and looked at me with big open eyes. He put his hands on his waist, sucked his teeth, and said in mock surprise, pretending he was like Ronnie Williams talking to Miss Lou. "But wait, look at this one here ... nuh!" I knew he was pleased with an answer I gave when he teased me, so I walked along contentedly.

Bredda Man stepped out onto the rocks along the river bed. He kept looking down into the water. He took some bits of hard-dough bread from his pocket and threw them into the water and watched them sink. He seemed to see something, which he took note of, and then walked on again.

"Yes, my little bredda, you see clear and true. Look at the grass and tell me what good it is, whether or not we have any use for it and know or believe in it."

I looked, and he stopped and stood beside me silently. I thought about what I saw. Swallows and little ground doves flew in and out of the grass over where the river sand crept into the bush. "Bredda Man, everything needs the grass. The Earth needs it to hold itself together. The birds, they need it for seed. The animals, they use it for food and shelter. The grass makes oxygen for us to breathe. Everything uses the grass."

Bredda Man nodded his head and said, "Now look at the river water and tell me what use it is, whether or not we believe or know it's there."

I chuckled because nobody in Jamaica would ever think they didn't need the rivers."The rivers feed the sea…they feed everything, Bredda Man. The eels that we feed on. The rain comes out of the sea. The rivers run into the sea and the entire Earth cools down because of the sea." I looked at him expectantly… it seemed so obvious to me but maybe I hadn't explained it clearly enough.

He nodded again and spoke. "What you say is true." He waved his hand to include everything we could see and continued. "It's the same with all Creation. What we believe, and the directions we walk, these concern us as human beings in our circle on the Earth Queen. But we don't consider what feeds on us, nor how we eat, as contributing to the Earth Queen's wholeness." He stopped at a big pond where we swam sometimes.

"Look at the river, maan." He asked me to tell him what I saw. I looked at the pond and I saw the water sparkling on the surface. He said, "Is that what you know the river to be?"

I answered, "that is what I know." The water looked so inviting. We walked on again and came to a waterfall.

Bredda Man stopped again. "Look at the river and see what's going on there, maan!" I looked at the waterfall and I noticed how fresh the rushing, gurgling bubbles were.

I told him, "I see a waterfall rushing along and falling powerfully, causing foam and churning up the pond."

"Is that what you know the river to be?" He asked again. I remembered the answer I had given to him before and realized there was more to his question than I had thought. I was silent as we walked on again, thinking about my answer. Now the river was passing over rocks at a shallow sand bed where it had to struggle in order to continue on its course.

We stopped again and Bredda Man looked. I looked, too, not needing to be told again. The river sand was glistening and when I looked deeper I saw every color of the rainbow. Before I could say anything, he walked on again and said, "We are food to something bigger than we know in any one part of our walk through life. That bigger knowing feeds upon our belief and partial knowing as we walk along the length of the river and learn more what its many forms and faces are. That is truth. We do this until we can know the river in all its forms, without believing the river is one form or another. That's what makes everything in Creation whole and know its place belonging here. When we have an understanding that our experience is only for this type of environment or that type of person, we cause a great wound in our understanding and we create isolation in our knowing. When we create this isolation, no matter how hard we try, we cannot see the whole picture."

I listened and was silent.

What did you learn from your bredda lizard?"

I was shocked, thinking that he somehow knew I had received the lizard's gift. I almost blurted out my experience. But I answered simply, "I learned to heal myself."

His eyes opened wide. Bredda Man looked at me intently, and the air became electric between us. He said, "In which part of your life do you feel that you can heal yourself because of the lizard's gift?" he asked.

This made me very uncomfortable again.

I replied, still confident he could not know that I had accepted the lizard's gift, "I feel it in our relationship."

He looked at me and asked, "then you are saying that the river is only the pool?" Puzzled, I scratched my head. He went on. "If healing is the gift you received, then to be true healing you must find a way to see the river of healing in all the different faces and forms it takes as your river of life winds its way through the forest. If the healing you received is true it must spread into every area of your life. When you become a healer, the gift is complete."

"But how will I know what to do when someone asks for help?" I asked.

"Lissen nuh, my little bredda, life shows us if we can pay attention to her Book of Life. Remember, 'When we can't hear, we must feel.' So when she asks us to listen to her and make changes, if we don't listen then we have to feel the consequences. Then we don't learn from what she tells us but from what we experience. Some of us wait till we get very sick to start to listen. If we are honest, we know she told us long before we got sick that things needed our attention but we refused to hear."

I was confused, but then I started to understand. "So when people need healing it means that they need the understanding that they have chosen to learn from feeling instead of listening to what life was telling them."

Bredda Man smiled and then went on, "That's exactly right. Whatever sickness we have becomes our teacher. Now your job as a healer is to help people to want to learn from their own life teachers … not to take those teachers away so they don't have to do their own work. No matter what you try to do, their work is their work. God does not negotiate as to whether we need to complete our work here … the only choice we have is how and when we complete it."

Bredda Man was silent. He walked on, watching the glistening water in silence. I felt my heart open in appreciation. I suddenly understood how each of the elements was part of a wholeness in creation. I realized I was a reflection of this wholeness and all that I knew in my life could be made to reflect the gift I had been given. I asked, thinking out loud, "so whatever gift a person is given by life, it's up to that person to make the gift whole in all of his life, not just one part?" Bredda Man snapped his fingers in the air again and smiled.

We continued our walk along the river. Bredda Man continued to drop morsels of bread and look into the water here and there on the way. Where we stopped again, the river was deep and flowed with a powerful force along steep banks.

Bredda Man nodded his head reverently. He spoke a blessing to the river. as he crumpled up some of the tobacco leaves from one of his shags and tossed them into the water. We watched them glide through the air for a few seconds, glinting in the Sun before they disappeared into the water.

"We are like the river, how it moves and flows. One place it is shallow, a next place it is deep, and yet still another place it is falling fast and furious, and the next place it stands up quiet and still. But all of these make the river, maan. And so that's how we are, too. We can only look where we are walking and feel the Sun on one side or the other. Knowing what we see is only part of wholeness is what makes us powerful. We feed this small knowing, our habitual perceptions to the bigger picture and not the other way around. We feed our seeing to the source of all light, the Sun. The more we feed life, the bigger the Creation that draws food from us and the more powerful we are."

The whole time he was speaking Bredda Man kept jumping up onto the rocks, dropping pieces of bread into the water and watching them sink.

Bredda Man had a way of making the world a magical place. I was beginning to see glimpses of a consistent thread—a holy thread that Bredda Man conjured both inside and outside—which runs through our hearts and joins us to the heart of Creation. I felt that Bredda Man and I were walking together on an ancient path. My own understanding and realization somehow completed what he said. A deep peace surrounded us.

I was stopped by a sudden density in the air. I had difficulty breathing. I could almost touch the air around me, it was so heavy. I looked up and saw a few John Crows circling overhead. One of them swooped down close to me. His powerful presence was majestic and ancient. His scent was to me sweet like a perfume. I remembered the beam of light that had descended over me at school during the May procession. I was filled with the same light again as I stood in his gaze.

I told Bredda Man, and he laughed, "Is only John Crow believe say him smell good!" But he also had a strange look in his eyes that made me believe he was thinking something else.

Bredda Man stood beside me in silence. Slowly the air thinned and became fluid again, and I could breathe normally again. Bredda Man's presence made it easier for me to return to my familiar awareness. He put his hand on my shoulder and said gently, "Now you understand that we are food to the big powers on the Earth. When we feed our individual habitual perceptions to a bigger knowing, to wholeness in our lives, we are ready to receive a living teaching from the Earth Queen. This is when we experience her as the Holy Land and she touches us with a living truth.

"These big powers, they are everywhere outside in the Wilderness, which is Creation, and they are inside of us. They feed off our understanding of wholeness. When we walk and hold nature dear to us, we feed the big powers. It's like a connection to the Sun in our heart. Our light ... the light we generate in understanding our lives as whole—like a river in which our gift flows unhindered—feeds the Sun. The Sun's light also feeds the Earth."

Bredda Man turned suddenly and headed off the path, disappearing into the bush. I could hear him slowly moving up the hill, and then it was silent. I was alone and I was still feeling very vulnerable. I felt the presence of the light again surrounding me. As I focused on it, my eyes were opened and I saw the whole of Creation from inside. This was the Holy Ground I walked upon with Bredda Man. I knew with every fiber of my being that we walked in a Holy Land of golden light together, where every tree and every bush, the river and the stones, the clouds and the Sun, myself and Bredda Man, all were part of this Holy Land! My heart felt like it would burst from the tremendous surge of warmth and yearning. I wanted to give my entire being to this Holy Land.

I lifted my hands up toward the Sun. I began to feel I was full of golden light and my hands moved because of the light, as if they were flames. Then I became still. I said "Thank you!" again and again as I stood surrounded by the grace of the sacred life to which I now recognize I belonged. I began to tremble. I had been devoured in the belly of beauty.

Slowly, I regained a more solid sense of my self. I felt that I was being watched. I looked up to see the John Crow observing me. He seemed like some dark-cloaked messenger. As I looked, he opened his wings toward the Sun with a gesture that was similar to what I had just been doing. Every hair on my body stood on edge. I realized he was showing me that he knew what I had done. I knew also in that instant that he, too, was aware of the Earth as the Holy Land. I felt I was in the presence of a Holy Being. I responded with a deep, respectful bow. Then the John Crow seemed satisfied. Our meeting was over. He turned and disappeared into the brilliant light of the Sun.

I stood rooted to the spot for a minute or two more in silence. I felt a sense of deep contentment. I was alone, but I was connected to everything. I was a tiny speck in Creation but I was also vast and spread out over all Creation. I was both the point and the periphery. Knowing this went hand in hand with knowing the Wilderness as the Holy Land. And this was not merely a thought, it was an experience. I felt different right down into my body now.

I moved slowly, like some giant mammoth, toward where Bredda Man emerged once again at the edge of the path.

He approached me with a satisfied look and said, "You remember what you were asking me about power? Now you know the first part of the answer."

"Now even though a man have money and be famous, him can still fall down because he is lonely inside…then the money and power cannot flow in there."

Bredda Man smiled again and stopped. He looked at me seriously and said in a tender voice, "Now listen my little bredda, that doesn't mean you can't be rich and happy too! It's not the money that directs the flow, it's the gift of understanding that uses the money. All that it means is that each of us have a responsibility to bring our gifts into wholeness on the Earth Queen."

Bredda Man became thoughtful and when he finally spoke, he said, "Listen nuh, John Crow, I am going to come back tomorrow morning to catch some of the eels down here. You may come and help if you want to."

After we walked our separate ways I suddenly realized Bredda Man had called me "John Crow." At first I felt proud to have been given a name by Bredda Man. But when I thought some more about it, maybe it wasn't that much of a compliment. John Crows were really not such handsome birds, and they ate rotting dead things. Then I remembered the ancient royal being in the golden light of my vision and I was reassured. I smiled affectionately. I felt that Bredda Man had answered my curiosity about my dream and told me I was now assigned the John Crow to learn from.

Just as I got home my cousins came out looking for me to go with them to the mall at Manor Park. When we got there I found a friend of Bredda Man selling "fry fish and bammy." A customer was complaining about the ugly John Crows sitting on top of a zinc roof nearby.

The old Rasta Man said, "No, Iyah, that is the king bird for his job is to clean the Earth Queen's Body. He is the high priest and the peacemaker among the birds for he never kills to eat. No sir, respect is due to that one, maan."

I was smiling proudly, but I still wasn't going to tell a soul my name was John Crow. I wasn't so sure I could live up to that lofty calling.

# 7

# The Eel's Gift

I WOKE UP WITH A START. It was still dark outside. The air was cool and crisp, but I was sweating. I had been dreaming again. Always the same. A black and a white figure are fighting. One wins by knocking the other down, then the defeated figure duplicates himself and returns to knock the other one down. This goes on and on until there is absolute chaos and huge numbers of both black and white figures fighting each other... then I wake up sweating.

I felt hung-over after the struggles of the night, but then I remembered about my arrangement to help Bredda Man catch eels. I jumped up, dressed quickly and headed for the kitchen. My mother was already baking something in the oven, which meant that there would be a big party at night!

"What are you doing up so early?" she asked.

"I'm going to catch some eels for your party!"

Her face lit up, "You know where to find them and how to catch them?"

I looked back at her with my hands on my hips and sucked my teeth—for added effect—to let her know that she was talking to *the* eel catcher of the Western world. She smiled as I slipped out the door and ran down the hill to meet Bredda Man.

I was feeling uncomfortable since I remembered Bredda Man saying that I should not eat eels because they were a distant part of the lizard's family. I wondered again if I should say something about my accepting the lizard's gift.

Bredda Man was waiting for me. He had a big empty white plastic bucket and a rolled-up newspaper with the bait inside. We walked to the storm gully and along the stony riverbed until the gully stopped at a small waterfall. Then we followed the river until we came to the same spot we had been the day before, where the bank was steep.

I watched as Bredda Man tied off the hooks and weights on the line. Then he baited the line with jonga (fresh water shrimp) and lowered it into the dark water.

In about a minute the line jerked. Bredda man watched quietly. The second time it jerked he deftly pulled the line up and away from the sharp rocks and the tangle of weeds on the bank. I saw a dark, writhing mass moving up the line. Suddenly an eel was in his hand. He slapped it smartly onto a big rock, first on one side and then on the other. The eel sprawled out, and stopped writhing. Bredda Man was very respectful of the creature as he took it off the hook and put it into the bucket where it lay curled up and still.

Bredda Man glanced at me. I was feeling guilty, thinking about how I would be betraying the lizard family. He looked at me and said. "What is medicine to you can kill a next man. What can kill a next man can be medicine to you. Everything can feed somebody and eel makes good medicine for they who suffer from nightmares and frighten easy. I know a woman who needs this medicine so that is why I ask you to come with me. Your bredda the lizard will bless this medicine because you are here."

I suddenly felt a whole lot better about catching the eels. "Can I catch them, too, then?"

Bredda Man looked at me and smiled. "Whatever you can use to help other people, as long as you respect it and live clean with it, that's all you need to concern your self with. Remember the eels in your heart. That is the way to honor them. Whenever you take something for food, remember where it came from. If you drink water, remember the clouds. If you eat meat, remember the animal it came from and imagine a next healthy animal, waiting to be born. The John Crow never wastes anything. Not even one drop of water. The John Crow never wastes a single thing…not paper…nor electricity. John Crow always embraces the big circle of life because he understands wholeness."

I wasn't sure I understood all of what Bredda Man said, but now I was really excited about catching one of the eels.

Before I could take up the fishing line, Bredda Man gave me some tobacco and motioned toward the eel in the bucket. When I sprinkled the tobacco on the eel I felt a strange sense of emptiness. Suddenly, my dream of the fighting figures came back to me. I felt disoriented and dizzy, and so nauseous that I had to lay down on the riverbank for a few minutes.

Bredda Man was watching me to see what I would do next. I got up and started to fix the line and hook. He nodded his head. But now the excitement and eagerness to fish for the eels was completely gone. Every movement I made was a huge effort. Bredda Man showed me how to use the line and bait it. I was still a bit dazed and I was nervous about the eel climbing up the line to get me, but I went ahead and dropped my line into the water.

In a minute I felt a jerk. I waited, not sure if I should pull up on the line or not. I felt another, stronger, jerk and the line was pulled hard. I pulled hard against it. My line snapped and flew out of the water without a hook or sinker, and without an eel.

Bredda Man watched quietly.

Still feeling strangely, I went through the motions of tying a new hook and sinker onto the line.

Bredda Man showed me with a quick, punchlike movement how the eels grab the food to pull it back into the rocks. Then he showed me how to time it just right to pull them up before they can get back into their holes and drag the line along the sharp rocks that would cut a line in two.

I tried again. This time I pulled up hard the first time I felt a jerk on the line.

A huge, writhing eel burst out of the water.

I jumped over onto a big rock. The eel was climbing swiftly up the line. He was watching me hold onto the line. As I looked into his eyes, I felt the strong pressure of responsibility in choosing to hurt him. It was like a burning inside.

But I saw in the eel's eyes that he had accepted his fate. He told me to go ahead and end my anxiety with a reverent attitude and respect for his gift.

I took hold of the eel and swung him in an arc over my head and slapped him down hard onto the rock. He didn't stop climbing up the line, so I slapped him down hard again. Finally, he lay still and limp. A single dot of blood came out of his mouth. I felt a peaceful acceptance of the gift the eel had made.

With great reverence and gratitude, I carefully took the hook out his mouth and laid him gently in the bucket. I voiced my feeling of "Thank you!" aloud to the eel.

"Aahiee!" Bredda Man said, "our breddas give life with respect, and when we take it with respect and reverence the cycle is complete."

We caught six huge eels between us, and then Bredda Man said it was enough. We could have caught many more eels, they seemed so willing to be caught. But there was no need.

There was no excitement or agitation as we took the eel gifts from the river. We asked in respect and we took in respect.

Bredda Man prayed over the water and sprinkled some tobacco into the river. He gave me some tobacco to sprinkle, too. We watched as it drifted for a while on the surface of the water and then disappeared downstream.

We cleaned the bank where we had been fishing and gathered up the remaining bait. Together we offered the bait to the eel family in thanks for their gifts.

Bredda Man threw the first jonga in and said, "Blessed river, there is one love in our hearts when we take these gifts to heal our people. There is one love in our hearts, Mother."

Then we rubbed our hands clean with river sand and rinsed them in the water. Bredda Man said, "Listen, John Crow, don't bother telling anybody where we caught them because the eels have to rest and grow back until next year. People may come who don't care and clean off the whole family."

I promised not to tell anyone where we caught the eels.

The bucket was too heavy for me to carry, so Bredda Man had to carry it all of the way back. When we came to the place to part ways, he tied two of the biggest eels onto a stick for me and reminded me, "Carry them with respect and speak with respect about them to honor their gifts."

Then we arranged to meet again later in the morning at the market.

When I got home, Alec, our farm manager, was working by the front gate. He looked admiringly at the two big eels. "Is where you find those big ugly somethings?" He asked teasing me.

I remembered what I had promised, and I also remembered that I was to honor the gifts of the lizard by remembering them with respect because they had given themselves to us with respect. I felt unsure how to convey my respect for them to Alec. I told Alec an old man traded them for my slingshot when I was out bird hunting.

"He stole your slingshot, eh?" Alec asked, implying the trade of my slingshot for the eels wasn't a good one.

I said to him, "No sir, they are good medicine to some people and they are a great gift the river gives us to heal with."

Alec looked at me seriously and was quiet. Then he nodded his head and smiled brightly. He looked at me with a glint in his eye. I realized he had been testing me. I blushed and hurried into the kitchen.

My mother and CeCe were hard at work in the kitchen. When she saw the two huge eels she was very impressed. I repeated the same story about the slingshot. I got a big hug from mom, while CeCe grinned her best mocking grin at me for not catching them myself.

I went upstairs to bed. Buck was still fast asleep. When I woke up again it was almost 9 o'clock. My brother was still fast asleep. I remembered about meeting Bredda Man at the market and leaped out of bed.

On the kitchen table, the eels were already peeled and filleted, their soft flesh laid out on foil, ready to be cooked.

CeCe knew about making medicine from the eel skin and heads. She had cut off the heads, skin and spines and was putting them in a pot outside to boil.

I just couldn't resist a poke as I left, "CeCe, is it true what they say the eels they taste better if you catch them yourself?" She grunted in a harried way, signifying she was busy.

Half way down the hill, as I was passing the construction site near the old Stinkin Toe tree, I spotted a big shiny motorcycle—an AJS Special. Some of the workers were standing around nearby. One of the young guys saw how interested I was and offered to show me how it worked.

The owner of the bike was the supervisor. He sauntered over and stood next to me. With a taunting look on his face, he asked me if I wanted to ride it. I knew he was mocking me, and I even felt that he would enjoy seeing me take a spill. But then I thought about how impressive it would be arrive at the market riding that beauty! I was feeling brave. So I answered seriously, "Yes!"

The guys all fell about laughing and joked, "Go on about you can ride the man's bike, maan! You can't even lift it off the stand, much less ride on it!"

The owner grinned and settled himself on top of a nearby wall to enjoy the spectacle. "Maan, gwaaan... take it off the stand and start her up!" he said, looking sideways at his friends, mocking my bravado.

I asked him, "Will you let me take it to Constant Spring and back?" The supervisor nodded his head, trying hard not to laugh.

I knew I couldn't push the bike off the stand myself but I figured once I got her started I could ride her right off. I turned the key and put all my weight behind the kick start. I was shocked when it started the first time. I revved the engine so loud that I let go of the throttle. All the workers were falling over with laughter. Then the bike began purring like a contented cat.

I sat up on the bike, my feet barely touching the ground, and rocked it forward and backward a few times until the bike rolled off the stand. I managed to stay on it and get it into first gear. The laughter suddenly stopped and the supervisor shouted from his perch on the wall, "What the rass clate do you think you are doing, boy?!" Before he could jump down, the bike took off with me on it. Everyone was chasing after me, shouting angrily, but I was too scared to look back because I thought I might tip over. I kept looking straight ahead, holding on, white-knuckled, for dear life, trying to steer the monster down the steep hill. Soon I couldn't hear the angry shouts any more. "A promise is a promise after all"…I chuckled to myself.

When I got to the dirt road I slowed down because I knew I had to be careful on the pebbly surface. I didn't remember in all the commotion how to use the brakes. I was also afraid to change the gears, so I just stayed in first. Luckily, by the time I got to the main road I had figured out about stopping.

At the junction I waited for a good clear run to make my turn out onto the main road. People driving by stared in disbelief at me sitting on that big old monster. On the main road down to Constant Spring I got up enough courage to change gears. The bike lurched a bit but then I felt I could go a little faster without the engine revving so high. I was already pretty confident when I got to the stop sign at the Golf course and I made a smooth, slow turn into the standing traffic. By the time I got to Constant Spring I was traveling in third gear.

I managed to get the bike over to a concrete wall where I put it into neutral and leaned it against the wall. Bredda Man saw me come in on the bike. He walked over casually, eating from a three-foot sugar cane strip he was carrying in a large crocus bag. First he told me that the eel medicine had helped the old woman and thanked me for helping to get it. Then he offered me some of the sugar cane. "Is that Maas Johnson's bike you riding?"

I smiled and told him the whole story. He laughed and said I had better take it back soon. Then he changed his mind and said he would ride with me.

I expected him to get in the front but he said to me, "You drove it down here …so you goin to drive it back!"

He held the bike until I was on it and had turned it out into the street, and then he hopped on the back and put the bag of sugar cane on his lap. I felt really proud in front of everyone in the market place by letting me drive with him as my passenger.

When we got to the dirt road, a carload of workers from the construction site pulled up beside us. They had obviously been chasing around trying to find me. From the looks on their faces they were not happy. But when they saw Bredda Man they quieted down and followed closely behind us as I drove back to the construction site. Maas Johnson was waiting there. He was hopping mad.

Bredda Man got off the bike first and said, "Alright, Maas Johnson, my little bredda carried me to bring you some sugar cane for lending him your bike. He said you bet him he couldn't reach market and buy sugar cane before it was time for your lunch!"

Maas Johnson looked puzzled. He hesitated, and then accepted the sugar cane. He felt like he had been shown respect and now he could afford to be good-hearted. He turned to the workers and said, "Look at what this little ginal brought for us, Rass clate, the boy is good." They all laughed. Maas Johnson paid Bredda Man for the cane and shared it out to all the workers. He was definitely back on top of the crew again.

Bredda Man and I walked down the hill together. He asked me, "What made you want to prove something to Maas Johnson? Is it trouble you are lookin for, nuh?" Bredda Man looked into my eyes. I did not know how to answer him, so we walked on to his cottage together in silence.

When we got to the cottage he sat down on the steps and lit a shag. I sat down beside him. He said, "You believe you alone can defeat all the mean-hearted people in this world?"

I did not understand his question fully, but it made me uncomfortable.

"What did you feel like when he said you could ride the bike?"

I jumped in to defend myself. "I knew he was mocking me and I believed he wanted me to fall off."

Bredda Man nodded his head silently. "So you wanted to prove he couldn't mock you and win. That gave his feelings power over you already. Whenever the mockin bird sings… you dance…isn't that how it goes?"

I felt naked again as I realized Bredda Man was right. I suddenly felt my antics were meaningless and that I had not proven anything at all.

"Before you decided to react and dance to the mocking bird's tune, what did you feel?" The question sent a shock way through me when Bredda Man asked me this. I saw a thousand reasons dance like embers flying into the air when a stick is thrown into a fire. Each of those embers was an agitated excuse or a defensive reaction to the pain that burned continuously inside.

I was trembling with the burning urge to defend myself against Bredda Man, but when I looked into his calm eyes I couldn't bring myself to argue with him. He smiled and waited until my intensity burned itself down.

Bredda Man was silent for a long while, which made me even more uncomfortable. I was relieved when he finally spoke again. "Get up!" He said firmly.

I stood up, wondering what we were going to do.

"Now bend down and touch your toes and hold on to them!"

As I bent forward and held my toes, I experienced a sharp pain in my hamstrings and lower back. I stood up immediately.

"So, what does the pain feel like?"

I replied, with great conviction, "It feels really bad."

Bredda Man nodded his head. "All right then, this time go down again and keep holding on."

I did it, more cautiously this time, but the pain was even stronger than before. As I was about to let go he said, "Now breathe into the pain and hold on to it."

But I couldn't bear the pain and I let go without trying to breathe. When I looked at Bredda Man he was staring into my face with a look of concern.

I bent over again. When I felt the pain I started to breathe, really forcing loud breaths into the pain.

Bredda Man came over to me and put his hand on my back. He said calmly, "Take your time and breathe and imagine the pain is your friend. Just imagine the pain is a very good friend and you're glad in your heart to know him."

I was confused, but I hurried to carry out the instructions so I could let go as soon as possible. As I breathed deeper and more smoothly my heart relaxed into a more accepting state.

"Close your eyes and listen. How is that feeling before you react to it?" I closed my eyes and the feeling that burned inside, became uncomfortable again. As I observed this fire burning inside me, I felt like it would devour me unless I moved or acted in some way. I was starting to fidget awkwardly.

Bredda Man said calmly, "Hold on to it, maan…don't make it chase you.… You don't have to fix anything nor react.… Look at it calmly and know you don't have to do anything at all … just look at it and feel it in your heart my little bredda. Now, let it expand to your whole body … that is your whole body awareness. Now feed it to your whole body awareness."

I grew calmer as I listened to his voice. An image came into my mind. I saw myself feeling CeCe's moods and knowing the violence that would follow. I saw myself unable to escape as I watched the image that ran like an old movie on my inner screen. Though the image lasted only a few seconds, it made me lurch forward. I felt the fire inside again grow stronger. I wanted to get up and move, so I opened my eyes.

Bredda Man's face was totally peaceful. He motioned to me to close my eyes again. I fidgeted nervously but managed to regain a sense of stillness. As the feeling surged up again, I thought that I was in real danger of pulling a muscle.

Bredda Man spoke again, "Pay attention to what is going on and breathe into it."

I started to breathe into the pain inside. But I felt the same powerlessness consuming me and I started to feel more agitated than ever.

Bredda Man spoke again, "Now breathe into the agitation and accept it is your bredda who has come to teach you. Don't run from your bredda. Take him into your house. Feed him to your whole body awareness."

As I ignored the impulse to escape into movement or become defensive, again the same images flashed into my mind and made me feel powerless. I decided to focus my attention on my whole body awareness. As soon as I did, a deeper image emerged, which I could hardly recognize, but its power scorched my memory.

In my mind I saw myself as an infant, totally vulnerable. A dark shadow was looming over me. I recognized the two figures of my dreams, the black and white figures. I sensed the dark figure as a great fear. I saw the fear devouring me. I watched as it slowly started to eat away at the white being and I was helpless to do anything about it. The image was too strong to hold on to. I opened my eyes.

Bredda Man asked me what I saw. I told him about the images of CeCe and the shadow I had seen.

He told me to move around, to start dancing. He said to pay close attention as I moved into the whole body awareness

I had just been practicing. I was glad to be able to move. As soon as I began to move I felt the memory of what I had seen receding. But I knew that feared image was not totally gone.

Then Bredda Man stood up and showed me a stance—the Earth Rooting stance, he called it. He planted his feet about two shoulder widths apart and sat on the air as if he were riding a horse. He beckoned for me to join him.

Then he started to push his open hands, palms out, in punching movements. I copied his movements, and we started to go faster and faster until we were in a smooth rhythm. He told me to do the movements as powerfully as I could, until I could feel my whole body awareness come alive. I copied him until I could feel my entire body merge with the energy in a rhythm of its own.

Then he suddenly shouted, "Stop!" I was breathing hard.

He said, "This time when you go back in your stance, remember your vision and give it to your body to use."

I wasn't clear about his instructions, but before I could say anything I was back in the stance, following his movements again. I held the awareness of my entire body as I started the punching movements again.

As soon as I felt my rhythm going smooth and strong again, I remembered his instruction to bring the vision into my whole body awareness. I faltered when I remembered the intensity of the impotence and fear I had felt. The heaviness frightened me and I lost the rhythm. Everything stopped.

Bredda Man waited for a while, and then we started again. I was still afraid of the vision. I followed his movements somewhat more timidly. We stopped again. "How long are we going to do this, Bredda Man?" He observed me closely and asked. "How does your body feel now?"

I felt heavy and tired, like I was carrying a big weight. But I said, "OK!"

Bredda Man watched and waited. I realized he was not accepting my answer. I decided to look inside again and be honest. I said, "I feel heavy and tired like I lost a fight."

Bredda Man looked ferocious and said, "Good!" and whipped his hand in the air. "You see, that feeling, that is the one that weighs you down. It's what you're doing when you hide that vision from your whole body awareness. Remember when you were touching your toes and felt pain in your body and you felt it was your enemy?" I nodded.

"Then what happened when you saw the pain as your friend and you accepted the teaching it brought to you?"

I realized that I had seen the powerful images when I had turned my attention inward. When I fed the images to an expanded physical awareness, my whole body awareness, I accepted the pain as a teacher instead of rejecting it and pushing it outward in aggressive movement and agitated talk.

"I saw the images that make me feel bad," I said.

Bredda Man spoke again, more calmly now, "You've learned to accept the gift of the body, now it's time to accept the gift of the imagination. Accept the images you see and give them to your whole body awareness to use. That is what you do every day without realizing it. You are using your body as a mule to carry around all the heaviness that is the imagination's gift."

I was dumbfounded by the realization that I really did carry this feeling of heaviness around with me in my body each day. "Will it make a difference if I choose to accept it as a gift rather than just riding on the mule?"

Bredda Man smiled. He was happy whenever I picked up on his instructions and guidance. "Come, let us do it again!"

We took up our stances, and I started pushing my hands out. The heaviness and inertia of my emotions was almost paralyzing me. I saw for the first time my emotions as a weight I was carrying around, instead of choosing to give it to my whole body awareness to use. I willed myself to push harder and faster. I remembered the images at the root of the heaviness. I held them. I remembered my whole body awareness and then, almost immediately, the rhythm I had established became deeper and more fluid. I felt a wave of emotional power animate my movements like an adrenaline rush. I willed myself to maintain the power and speed of the movements within my whole body awareness. The movements became effortless and I moved now powerfully and fast in an unshakable rhythm beyond my own familiar physical capability.

Bredda Man noticed the shift in my awareness and stood beside me. "Give it to the whole body to use. Make the body talk for those feelings and images. You don't have to speak. Make the whole body say everything."

I experienced a deep emotional catharsis as wave after wave of grief and anger flowed through my body. I wanted to shout, but I remembered what Bredda Man said, "Make the whole body say everything."

I put the emotion into the movements and whole body awareness instead. Then I experienced a sensation of great clarity, and felt as if my entire body was light as a feather. My awareness expanded and everything around me became a part of who I was at that moment. The ground disappeared. I felt a union with the elements. It was as if there was a natural process, like a whirlwind, happening in the spot I was standing. The sky, the animals, the air, deep space, all was part of that moment, of who I was. I felt all that I was experiencing was part of the Circle of Life. I did not want to stop. The movements naturally slowed down. I was amazed at how clean and fresh my body felt after working so hard.

I don't know how long I had been dancing in my trance-like state, but Bredda Man had made tea and prepared some food for us. I walked over to where he sat sipping tea and he handed me a dish of cold ackee and salt fish. I did not feel hungry or thirsty but he said I should eat something. As I ate, my hunger came back and I found myself wolfing down the last scraps of food on the plate. I do not remember ever feeling as light or as clean inside as I did then.

"What happened?" I asked him.

He drew on his shag and blew the smoke toward me. I patted it into my body as he had taught me to do. "You used the gift of imagination consciously … that's all. Instead of seeing it as your enemy, you accepted it as your friend. Whenever you face your friends you can receive the gifts they carry for you. That is when each one of our friends becomes our teacher. Your agitation does not have to be the catalyst for carelessness and bravado. You can use it to understand the wholeness of your being. In using your imagination consciously, you choose to feed your agitation to wholeness instead of chaos."

Then Bredda Man drew a circle on the ground with four equal arms coming out from the center to the circumference.

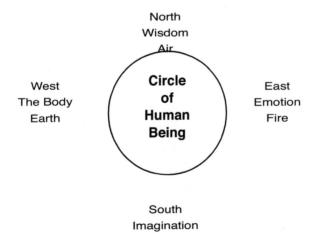

### Water

"There are four friends we have that most people regard as enemies—the Body, Imagination, Emotion, and Wisdom."

As he spoke he pointed out each element as a direction on the circumference.

"These four make up the circle of our humanness. When we treat them as enemies, we can't receive the gifts they carry for us. Now you've learned how to accept the gifts from two of your friends—the Body and Imagination. You've allowed them to become your teachers. There are two others of the circle for you understand—Emotion and Wisdom. Remember, these friends are always there for you. When one brings a gift that you find difficult to accept, there is always another there who will help you to receive that gift. That's the wisdom of using the circle. Knowing how to move around it, and in and out of it."

After eating and drinking, I was feeling content. Bredda Man blew some more smoke over me and sent me home. In my heightened state of awareness, I bounded toward home. I felt my skin was a thin, permeable film separating my being from everything around me.

I began walking more slowly because now I was starting to get more and more confused about what Bredda Man had said. And then it came to me—by moving into the physical realm of walking I could call on the friend of the West to help me with the challenge of the friend of the North to understand the wisdom teachings. I also realized that by simply shifting my awareness to a different level I could allow answers to come because I was less tense.

I was passing by the construction site just then, and all the men smiled at me and shouted out in a friendly way. "Respect, little bredda, respect!" I waved my hand and smiled to them. I felt they were friends now. Maas Johnson looked at me with a cautious but genuine smile. I wanted to apologize to him for the pride I had felt in defying him, but his warm smile told me it was not necessary.

That night, lying in bed, I thought about the day. I recalled the experience I had with the eels and how my nightmare came to me when I offered the tobacco from Bredda Man's shag to the eel. I saw that was part of the eel's gift—helping me to remember. I thought about the four enemies, and how I had turned two of them into friends and teachers. I also thought about how calling on one friend within the circle could help me with a challenge from another one. I wondered about the two other enemies—and friends—I had yet to meet.

# 8

# The Teaching of the Plumb Line

THE NEXT DAY my cousin Jason came to visit. He wanted to show me how to drive a car. Lucky for us, the perfect opportunity presented itself. His mom and my mom were out on a shopping trip together and our car was sitting in the garage.

We spent the morning driving around near the house. When Jason thought that was getting boring, he decided we should go for a longer adventure. Before I could protest, he was halfway down the driveway. And that is where our luck ran out. When we got to the dirt road at the end of our driveway, a police car was parked there. One of the officers was chatting up a girl who worked at the apartments there. Jason sat up straight and tall, trying to pretend it was OK for him to be driving. But the policeman took one look at us and jumped into his car as we tried to pass by.

Jason took off. I told him we should stop, but he was too intent on getting out onto the paved road. I knew the roads much better than he did and I said we should stay on dirt roads because they were harder to chase us on. I directed him onto a dirt track that skirted a long field, where the dust from our tires would make it really hard to follow us. But soon we could see the lights of the police car flashing sporadically in the dust cloud that billowed across the increasingly shorter distance between us.

I was nervous because I knew the dirt track would soon come out onto a main road, so I shouted for Jason to make a sharp left turn down a very narrow dirt path that led to a steep gully and then to another road back home. The police car tore past as we made our sharp left turn. We sped on and almost flew into the gully before we saw the small dirt track on the left and screeched around the corner. When we got back to the dirt road that led to my driveway, we parked the car off the road and waited nervously, until we were sure that the police car wasn't coming back. Then we drove the car slowly the rest of the way home. We had to spend the rest of the afternoon cleaning dust off the car. It was everywhere.

I was upset by Jason's carelessness and wildness. I said I felt sorry that we had almost gotten ourselves into bad trouble. And also I didn't care for the thrill of the car chase as much as he did. I preferred the woods and spending time with Bredda Man. Jason was soon bored with the clean-up part, and he left me to finish it.

When my mom came home. The garage floor was all wet. She looked at her shining, clean car and asked who had done such a good job washing it. Just then Jason conveniently appeared and tried to pounce on the opportunity to get the credit for a good deed. I didn't feel we deserved it, so I said someone came by. My mom gave me some money to give to him, That would work just as well for Jason, who wanted to take the money and buy cigarettes. When I wouldn't let him have the money, he got mad at me and left.

Later on in the day, I met Bredda Man. He was sitting in the shade smoking his shag. I told him the whole story. He looked serious and said it was a good thing we didn't get hurt, or hurt anyone else either.

Bredda Man called me to sit down beside him. "Listen nuh, John Crow, when we young we believe we can fly before we can walk. Whatever we imagine must come true, if we imagine it long enough. And when we imagine things that are careless they will come true, too, just like the good things we can imagine to help our family and ourselves.

"When we imagine things long enough, we forget we have created them. Some people even believe, whatever happens to us has nothing to do with the fact that we imagined it into reality. When somebody tells us what is going on, we can't see it or believe it. When we have imagined something for a long time so that it becomes real and then mistakenly believe it's something that just happened by itself... that is slavery, maan."

Then he asked, "Remember when you felt heavy after your dreams?"

I nodded my head.

"Imagine if you never faced your enemy and made him your teacher. What would happen to your body if you carried around that heaviness for a whole lifetime?"

I shook my head to acknowledge how miserable the prospect seemed to be.

"Before you knew the teaching, the two friends them bring to you and how it makes your body feel, did you think say it would be hell?"

I realized I would never have thought about the possibility of using my body to change my emotional state. I shook my head again and sighed. Bredda Man was right. I would not have believed living with that heaviness was hell, I would just have told myself, like so many people do, "That's life!"

"What made you want to follow your cousin to do his mischief?"

I did not know how to answer.

I stuttered trying to make sense. "I…I…didn't really want to … I just got caught up in the drama of life…that's all."

Bredda Man shook his head and said, "Listen, nuh, it's practice of being careless that makes you not know what you're doing and makes you a follower. Get up again and take up your stance."

I jumped up, happy to get off the hot seat. Bredda Man showed me some new movements. They looked like a mixture of martial arts and dance. He called them the Guardian Pattern. I struggled trying to copy him because the movements were unfamiliar. After showing me a combination of movements four times, he stopped and asked "How does your body feel?"

"It feels funny, uncomfortable. It wants to know how to establish a rhythm so I can do the movements."

Bredda Man laughed and said. "Every one of the elements has a story. The body tells a story. How we know the body and each of the elements in our circle, either as enemy or friend, makes our story meaningful to the world.

"Habit is the nature of knowing for the body. The body always wants to maintain the story it already knows. Whenever we try to learn something unfamiliar, the body has to suspend its habitual postures and way of moving until it learns the new movements. Then the body can add them into its familiar routine … its familiar posturing. To understand the four ways of the "enemy" teachers we have to start with the body first.

The pattern I am going to show you is a guardian pattern. The teaching is all about knowing how to learn and how to protect the pattern from identifying with habit. The pattern is about Life. It also is the deepest Knowing. This teaching is to protect the deeper Knowing pattern from forgetfulness and habit. If we do it right, we do it in perfect silence and stillness.

Then the deeper pattern will reveal itself. Now focus entirely on the senses and learn by imitation... and don't ask questions."

"But how can I move and also maintain silence and stillness, Bredda Man?" I blurted out.

He smiled, but did not answer. Then he started to do the movements again. I still felt a stubborn insistence on having a verbal explanation. But when Bredda Man finished, I realized his movements were my explanation.

The way to learn in this guardian pattern was to be entirely focused on the bodily senses. When Bredda Man moved he was totally absorbed in the movements he was doing. His movements had a power about them that came from being totally present and focused. There was nothing else that concerned him when he moved, nothing but his movements. He was totally committed to his dance.

When I could really learn by imitation, without the distracting need for explanations or justifications for what we did, I would be really attentive and clear. Bredda Man smiled and began the pattern again. I began to copy him, totally absorbed in the minute details of each movement. But my mind still wanted to ask questions. Each time I felt a thought arise I would start to fall out of rhythm with him, and I would have to check myself and focus on the movement again. Then I regained my step in harmony with his movements. As I disregarded my own need to ask questions, I lost the need for an explanation. Because I did not ask my question I felt a trust build between us in the silence. Then I could follow him without missing any of the details. He turned to me and smiled. "That is good.... You have learned to pay attention."

"This teaching concerns the third and fourth friends: Emotion and Wisdom. When we don't know our own heart we are easily drawn into this or that argument. When we can't read our own four elements in silent stillness, accepting the gifts they bring, how can we accept the gifts in other people's Emotions and Wisdom? We tend to see other people's Emotion and Wisdom either as an advantage to us or as a threat. But the gift of the friend Emotion is to protect the still, quiet heart. That is the gift of the One Heart—the Formless Heart.

"In guarding the silent Knowing in the heart we learn to be wise. Whatever we feel in our hearts, whether good or bad, is a gift. When we say this Emotion is good and that one is bad, we are fighting against our own heart. When we establish wholeness in our being, what we feel is neither bad nor good. It simply is. The first step is to see Emotion as energy and stay focused with it until it becomes our friend, no matter how intense the energy is.

"The gift of Wisdom is in trusting the quiet knowing inside, which is invisible. At first this quiet inner knowing may seem less powerful than the rantings and raving of careless, loud people. But each time we trust this inner knowing, we become less tied into other people's dramas. And the more we trust it, the more our own Wisdom emerges."

As we prepared to dance the pattern again, Bredda Man turned to me, "Whenever you make mistakes in the pattern, stay still and quiet. Observe the mind wanting to fix things and change the focus away from the body. Whenever the mind wants to start chasing this idea or that question, focus on the movements. If you make mistakes, stop and focus on the body in stillness. Stay quiet.

"No matter what the mind tells you, don't follow the impulses of your thoughts…. Keep still, until you know how to continue. That is the reflection of not asking questions outside. The teacher inside and the teacher outside know we are ready to learn by our stillness and relaxation."

I nodded my head eagerly.

"Now do the pattern again, without believing it is uncomfortable to learn something unfamiliar."

I was unsure what he meant. I felt agitated because I wanted so much to understand, but my body objected—this desire to know felt uncomfortable. Then I understood what he meant. I would try to stay with the feeling of the desire without believing it was bad or uncomfortable. I would just feel it and let it be as I learned the movements. I copied him again and focused on the feeling of agitation in my body. When I did not allow the agitation to become something bad or uncomfortable, as I followed his movements, a shift occurred. I felt the cleanness in my body again as I let the energy flow without allowing it to be a discomfort. What I had labeled discomfort before I now felt as energy.

Bredda Man smiled and asked me, "What you body feel like now?"

I replied spontaneously, "I feel really alive, Bredda Man!"

He nodded and said, "You see how easily you answered this time. When we keep our awareness in the energy level we do not have to identify it as good or bad. Whenever we identify our energy as good or bad, comfortable or uncomfortable, we get stuck and we cannot react spontaneously."

I understood what he said when I saw how clearly I had answered his question this time without any hesitation or stuttering.

Bredda Man spoke again, "Come make we do it again. You soon know the pattern now. Then make me see you do it by yourself."

We went through the pattern together until I was comfortable that I could do the movements myself. After I had gone a few steps on my own, Bredda Man shouted at me to stop. He said I was doing it all wrong.

I dropped my hands. Now I was confused. "I thought I was doing it right."

Bredda Man was still and waited silently, watching me very intently. Suddenly I remembered what he said about being still and silent if I made a mistake. I realized he had tricked me. I laughed and shook my head. He remained absolutely still. Looking at his neutral expression and the total focus he maintained, I realized what I had to do next. I took up the pattern where I left off. I became still, waiting to remember where I went wrong, or for him to correct me.

Bredda Man said, "Now you are ready to learn."

He showed me the form again, and I copied the movements with him. Then he said I should do it again on my own. I started doing the form again.

He shouted "Stop!"

I stopped still and was totally silent as he watched me closely.

"You made a mistake again."

I felt confused and kept still. I let go of the form's posture I was holding and spoke out. "What did I do wrong?"

He watched me again and said I should pay attention to standing in a more relaxed pose.

Then he looked at me and asked, "So, what was the mistake you made?"

I did not know.

He waited until I had been silent for a while and continued. "How do you know you made a mistake?"

Then I realized he was tricking me again. He smiled and nodded his head. My eyes lit up and I wanted to speak but he continued before I could say anything.

"We give our authority away to people when we do not really know if what we are doing has meaning or not. When we look for validation without taking responsibility for the way we learn, we get confused. When one person tells us this and another one tells us that, we are more likely to give up what we are doing to join in their drama if what we are doing has no real meaning to us. It's the same thing as when you answered back because you did not really know whether what you were doing was truly correct. You went outside the discipline to validate your uneasiness."

I was beginning to know what Bredda Man was getting at.

"You are right, Bredda Man, I didn't trust what I knew and so I stopped concentrating. I hadn't really committed myself to the learning."

He nodded quietly and said, "Come make we do it again. This time do it with a focus on knowing what you are doing and not on making it comfortable."

As we danced through the form together again, I stayed focused on my own knowledge of what came next. I was not relying on following him. I made each movement my own. When we finished, I realized we had remained in perfect time and step, all the way through. I felt I took ownership of the form by staying focused on my own knowing.

"How does your body feel now?" he asked quietly.

"I feel like this is my dance now."

Bredda Man nodded his head and motioned for me to do it on my own. I moved forward and began. I kept my attention totally focused on knowing and observing every detail with care and attention. This time, when I finished and he was silent and nodded his head. "That is life, my little bredda … that is life! Now what does your body feel like?"

"My body feels fresh and alive and I feel open."

Bredda Man answered with his familiar "Aiyihee!"

We danced for well over an hour, and we both were sweating. Bredda Man stopped and picked a couple of oranges off a nearby tree, and we sat down together to enjoy the sweet juicy pulp. He said, "When we stay focused on the silence in the heart, we reflect that silence and magnify it in all of our directions. The Formless Heart becomes a real guiding force in our lives."

Bredda Man looked up at me seriously and continued. "Your cousin Jason is going on like a wild dog. You think Jason doesn't respect you if you don't go along with him?"

I remembered how contemptuous Jason was when I wouldn't go along with his schemes.

"You followed him because you are not sure of your own form yet. If you stay focused on your own knowing, what would you do when Jason wanted you to come with him?"

I responded quickly, "It's like doing the form, if I know it, I won't doubt it, even when someone else tells me I am wrong. And I won't do things simply because somebody else says it's a good idea. I will trust my own knowing. I am beginning to understand how the four gifts work."

Bredda Man went on, "You really believe Jason knows what he is doing? What happens if one day Jason knocks down somebody and kills him?

I realized Jason was not really aware of his carelessness. Something about his fearlessness had impressed me. But now that I looked inside at my own knowing I saw his behavior was foolish.

Now that I could see the value of my own knowing when I was doing the dance pattern, I could see that the trust I placed in my own movements made my body feel better than when I looked for validation from Bredda Man's movements. The situation between Jason and me was similar. I had to learn to trust my own pattern and emotions rather than go along with his. I realized the agitation I felt around Jason was his own interpretation of his heart energy, which was full of fear and recklessness.

But that was still not the end of it because if I hadn't the same recklessness and fear inside me as Jason did, I would not have been drawn to him! I thought about this side of myself in relation to doing the form, and I saw clearly how fear and recklessness wanted to assert themselves in me so I would not learn. If I didn't keep to my commitment and follow the guidelines that I knew would help me, then the fear and recklessness would win. Like Bredda Man said before, "If we can't hear…we must feel!"

Bredda Man went on, "So when you join in with somebody and deny your own knowing, you're losing your self and you practice carelessness. That's why this dance is called a guardian pattern. It's about learning to protect what we know is right.

"We check in with our Emotions during the dance by asking, 'How do I feel?' We keep in touch with our Heart and Wisdom because they are our friends and we want to show we care in a consistent way. We don't wait until there is a disaster to check up on our feelings."

Bredda Man shook his head and said sadly, "When we practice carelessness, following this impulse and that one, we make our discomfort become real and we deny our deeper knowing. It's like when you imagined that your feelings were bad. They were just energy inside…energy you could use if you just let it be, without any judgment. Is our impulsive, careless side that wants to know everything right away. We have to get answers now and so we make everything black and white, good and bad. Once we magnify this carelessness in acting on it, it is harder to make decisions based on our own unique knowing. That is why so many people feel lost and wild, because they eventually lose touch with what they know as real. When someone asks us about our true self, we feel lost and confused because we have ignored knowing it for so long."

"I am going to tell my mother what happened with the car, Bredda Man!" I said triumphantly.

Bredda Man appeared unimpressed. He bent down to tie his shoelace as if I had not spoken at all. I felt let down. I waited to see if he would respond to my noble gesture.

Bredda Man just smiled—a cool, wry smile. He shrugged his shoulders and dusted off his pants as he stood up, and then he walked off without speaking a word. At the gate he turned and shouted that he would see me again in a few days.

Without Bredda Man's approval, I felt abandoned. I lost the will to carry through with my plan. Then I thought about what Bredda Man had said. I decided to choose to see the Emotion I was feeling as energy and not to identify it as painful or embarrassing.

As I focused my attention inside I imagined I was doing the form again. I realized Bredda Man had given me a gift. By not choosing a direction for me, by ignoring my impulsiveness and my desire for approval, he had allowed me to realize the benefits of choosing my own good-heartedness myself. I felt elated because now I was beginning to trust my own knowing.

Then I thought about my relationship with Jason, and again I was unsure about trusting my decision to do the right thing. But again there was no one to validate or support my choice. I was on my own and I felt lonely. Then I realized that there were two paths out of my loneliness. In one, I could choose to be defensive and isolate myself from everyone and deny my knowing. In the other, I could choose to use the Wisdom teachings and create a more open world for myself.

As I looked at this Emotion from the energy level, I saw my fear of being alone if I chose my own path over Jason's. I could lose Jason as a friend. But I also saw that going along with a friendship that dismissed my own knowing was no friendship at all. I continued to stay with the energy level of the Emotion until a deep warm trust began to rise up inside my heart. I felt my heart had truly become my friend. In that moment of grace I did not need any other company. I felt that I had the best friend in the world—Myself.

I decided no matter what anyone else thought, I would do what I thought was the right thing. I went to my mom and told her the whole story. She was concerned and annoyed but she wasn't angry. She told me I would always have to ask permission to use the car. Jason was grounded for a week.

Jason didn't like what I had done one bit. He came by a few days later, driving his mother's car, and asked me if I wanted to go for a spin. His eyes looked empty and mean. I checked my heart and I heard "No!" I tried to speak to him in a kind and honest way, but he was dismissive of my attempts.

I asked Jason, "What happens if you knock somebody down, maan, or you get hurt?" He looked at me and smirked. Then he floored the gas pedal so that the wheels spun and made a whole lot of dust. I had to jump back from the car. But I felt calm and centered as I watched him speed off down the road, careening wildly from one side to the other.

I saw Bredda Man again a few days later, and he smiled when he saw me. He knew I had told my mother the story. I felt my own smile warm my whole face and chest when I saw him. I just had to ask him if I had done the right thing. He didn't answer me, but he chuckled as we walked toward the forest together. I immediately realized I was seeking approval again. Then I smiled, knowingly, at his mischievous giggle.

When we got down by the gully where the river was dammed up, he picked up a stone and took a piece of fishing line out of his pocket. I watched quietly as he sat and tied the fishing line around the stone.

"Look here, John Crow! You know what this is?"

I looked at the stone hanging down at the end of the line and shook my head.

"This is plumb line. Is what was used to help build houses a long time ago. Today, is the same idea used in the spirit level."

Then I remembered seeing the builders down the road use them to level the walls and floors as they worked.

Bredda Man gave the stone a slight push. The pendulum swung back and forth in shorter and shorter arcs as it tried to regain its balance. We watched the stone until it returned to stillness.

Bredda Man held the stone out to one end of the pendulum's arc and looked into my eyes.

"Yes, John Crow, one end of its swing represents our negative attitudes and the other end is our positive ones. In between is nothing. You see that is when the pendulum rests in the zero. That is when it reads true. That represents knowing our true self. Is like when you feel helpless and want approval on one side. The other side is when you defy you own heart because you get mad that nobody will help you."

Bredda Man continued calmly, letting the pendulum swing. He caught it at the other end of the swing and held it as he spoke, "You say you want to be truthful. But one day you get excited about this and believe the whole world is full of things to teach you and the next day maybe you say the world is against you."

I realized he was illustrating his point with each movement. Bredda Man saw my understanding and continued. He let the stone go again and it swung back through the center to the other side of the arc. He did this several times catching it at each side as he continued to speak, until he was satisfied that I saw that what he was saying was reflected in the swings of the pendulum. He looked at me and nodded his head approvingly and went on.

"The wise person inside us is still, like the center of the pendulum. This wise person asks, 'If you want to be truthful, how can I believe someone who says each time that how I feel today is the way the world has always been? If I am to believe you are sincere, which truth should I accept, the one when you are open and receptive to the world as a place to learn or the one where you say the entire world is against you?'"

"So," Bredda Man said, "which is the real truth? Should we simply accept that we have no truth rooted in our being because we want to impose our contradictory perceptions onto all time and space? This is how we learn to trust ourselves... by understanding the knowing of the center in ourselves. We don't have to believe the right or left swings that want to paint all time and space with the brush strokes of polarity."

Bredda Man let the pendulum swing to the other side before he caught it and looked at me to see that I was following him before he continued. I wasn't at all sure what he meant, but I sensed a big lesson was around the corner. Bredda Man's teachings often came like a storm ...a mounting build up of clouds and wind before the soothing release of the rains came.

"Now, inside each of us is a still knowing. That one listens to both sides, one side tells the still knowing 'the world has always been this way, hard and cold.' The other side tells the still knowing 'the world is beautiful and nice.' Whether we are in the right or the left side of the swing, we are totally identified with the eternal aspect of that side. But that is a dilemma, because we know that we cannot remain in the eternally absolute of either side. Which one do you think is the right way?"

At first, I couldn't decide. Then it slowly began to dawn on me that there was no way a wall could be raised up straight, if either side of the plumb line's arc was set as the line to base a building upon. The only way to find a straight line from the ground up, was to follow the still center of the plumb line. I wasn't sure whether my realization was an answer to his question. I stuttered, without any confidence, "Neither… neither one…. I mean, we should not believe either the right or left because our still center is the only accurate one to base the building upon."

Bredda Man's eyes opened wide and he looked at me in mock disbelief. He laughed right out loud and slapped my shoulder and shook me gently, roaring with delight. Then he stopped and waited as if the answer was only half baked. I started to feel confused again, so he went on.

"My little bredda speaks true. It is the center we follow if we want to build something that will last. When we listen to either side we cannot know truth until the heart is still in silence. That is how we empower our center, by listening to it. That is when we become trustworthy, when we stop projecting our judgements of right and wrong, black and white, happy and sad, out into time and space. When the drama stops and the heart settles into the silence…that is when we know the center has a voice. That is when we learn to trust our own knowing and not just swing from one side to another."

I was beginning to understand what he meant.

"We can't trust ourselves till we find the center. How can we believe a person who swings to one side, says one thing one day, and the next day him say something opposite, and him believe both when him say so? See, this is what we do when we have no center. When we can't trust ourself. We go to learn demanding answers from our impulsive carelessness, and we don't trust the learning process unless we can control it. That is the swing to the right. Then when we don't get what we want, we don't get direction approval or judgment, we tell ourself, I was right not to trust this teaching. Then we choose to fall back on our old habits…being careless and acting impulsive. That is the swing to the left. See this is what these swings do. They make sure we never know the center. Nothing really changes, it only moves from right to left."

I realized that is how I had behaved most of my life…seeking validation and approval for what I wanted to do or how I felt. I never took responsibility for my feelings. I used peoples reactions to justify what I felt. When people liked my happy excited enthusiasm I felt that was good. When people were judgmental about my moodiness and anger, I felt that was bad. I never knew if my feelings were good or bad unless someone else liked or disliked them. Suddenly I saw these polarized swings as an oppressive mechanical process I was doomed to be subjected to for the rest of my life. I felt really heavy and sad.

I was dumbfounded at how simply Bredda Man had demonstrated with a string and a stone this world of swinging left and right.

Bredda Man continued speaking in his gentle voice, "How do we treat the two sides if we want to grow straight and true?"

I answered immediately, "We don't have to believe or act on them, until they come back to stillness. That is when we understand the center is always true. There we can remain true to watching and observing that we are just feeling bad or good, without identifying with either one."

Again, Bredda Man let the stone go. He caught it at the opposite end of its arc. Again, he looked into my eyes and said, "When we find the balance inside, and we don't care what anybody else thinks or believes because we know we are doing the right thing, we grow inside. We can still smile and be happy but we know it comes from our own sense of truth, which does not need someone else to make us trust that our happiness is real.

We can still feel sad and angry but we don't need anyone else in order to make us understand the gift of these feelings for us. We have no reference point except our own Heart Knowledge. It is the hardest thing for most of us to take our bearings from this plumb line of our own still and silent Wisdom. Nobody can teach us to trust our own Heart. When we stay honest and still in our energy, like the resting place of the plumb line, and not reacting against something, swinging from one side to the other, then we Know who we are and we Know nothing can change that stillness because it is true.

"In that still place there is only our honesty and conscience to guide us. When we lift ourselves up to hear our center in the midst of all kinds of confusion, we develop will. We become the straight measure. Our honesty becomes deep rooted. Even our ignorance cannot upset the balance.

"Knowing our Self at the center, we take time to establish our own understanding … we go beyond what we expect and assume, to realize our own conscience … then we can trust it. We develop substance, maan! That is what the man of knowledge needs, substance! You see how the building of character gets raised up?"

Bredda Man took up a stance and folded his arms. He motioned me and said, "I want you to move now that you know the pattern. Now look into your own Wisdom and move from there without wanting me to validate what you know. Move from a place of certainty. I don't mean pretend to be sure. I want you to trust your own stillness and feel it when you move."

I was confused and nervous. "I…I…am not sure," I started to speak, trying to stammer my way into the place he spoke about.

Then I remembered the rules of the pattern, stillness and silence. I realized in that moment I had to act, whether I was perfect or not, whether my understanding was right or not. I started to move and focused on keeping the energy awareness without judgement as I moved. I was observing my body as I wheeled and jumped, kicked and hit the air with my hands. I was perfectly still inside, although my body was moving full throttle. I finished. I stood still in the silence and looked into Bredda Man's eyes. He knew I had understood. I had showed him I knew exactly what he meant me to know.

I did not need Bredda Man's approval, nor should I seek it—even though I trusted him—for doing what I knew was right. When I looked to him for approval to do the right thing I was swinging to one side. When I did not get approval and doubted whether I was doing the right thing, I was swinging to the other side. Now that I saw both sides clearly I felt an intense energy building inside. It was a matter of learning to make decisions for myself that were wise and truthful from a place of balance within myself—the center of the pendulum swing. Moving through the form with a focus on the stillness inside had energized the balanced way of seeing my dilemma.

Bredda Man then asked me, testily, "So you know the pattern now?"

I did not answer, remembering that anything to do with learning the pattern meant we were under the rules of silence and stillness.

When he saw I was silently waiting for his next demonstration, he nodded his head and said, "Good!"

Then he approached me and said, "What we know in one part of the river of knowledge may feel complete. The seed contains the entire plant—the shoot, the leaf, the blossom, and the fruit—but without the work of the gardener, this knowledge might not find fertile ground and it would remain hidden and unfulfilled."

He motioned for me to repeat the pattern again. I did. "Now show me what the movements are for."

I thought they were for exercise. I had no idea the movements had any other application. Then Bredda Man showed me how each movement had an application in self-defense. I was amazed at how much more powerful the movements became when they were applied in this way. I felt a new sense of purpose and meaningfulness in my movements. After he taught me the self-defense applications until I knew them all, he asked me to do the pattern again. When I finished, he asked me again, "How does it feel this time, is it different than before?"

"Yes, my movements had more purpose."

Bredda Man smiled. "Now remember, you thought what you knew before was complete. And it was … but the same movements you learned before were the seeds that held this further knowledge inside. Until I showed you the applications, you could not harvest the fruits of this garden."

I laughed because of the way he spoke in allegories that helped me to understand so quickly.

"That is like life, our knowledge about this and that is not complete until we go deeper within and truly apply what we have learned. Many people learn the deepest secrets but because they never apply the knowledge in a meaningful and wholesome way it is wasted, despite the fact they believe it makes them special. Now… do you know the pattern?"

"Yes! I know it."

Bredda Man shook his head, smiling, and I immediately realized I should not have spoken so impulsively.

"Life is like the pattern—the same rules of stillness and silence apply all the time. This is the teaching of wholeness we have spoken about before. It's not just in one area to apply these teachings. If you think applying them in your pattern is the only place, you wound your own self-realization. You isolate your knowledge. You think in boxes and behind fences. Remember, if you are not sure, don't speak."

I was silent. He watched me again and then suddenly said, "Now you teach me the pattern and applications."

I was caught entirely off balance. I could not have ever imagined teaching Bredda Man something. In my mental panic I completely forgot the pattern.

He laughed again and reassured me. "Come on, try!"

I stood in front of him and could hardly remember where to start. He stood perfectly still and silent like a good student. I started to relax and after a while I managed to go through the entire pattern of self-defense applications with him.

When we finished he said, "Now do the pattern again."

I did the pattern with a new appreciation for it. It had become second nature now and I was a lot more confident of the details and my own posture.

When I finished he asked me, "How did it feel?"

I was amazed at the difference. Each time there was more to learning and knowing, I now felt a huge difference in the way I did the pattern.

"It felt different again. I will not ever again say that I know this pattern once and for all!"

"Now you understand that Knowledge is more than an assumption about what we have learned in one specific place and time. The river flows on and our knowledge should keep growing and deepening. Most of the time we are impulsive and careless about our knowledge. This modern culture teaches deep things like they are valueless dust. People believe we know things because we learned the first level of knowledge—by copying. Until we learn to apply our knowledge and then train others in it we remain in a fantasy world with our knowledge."

I stood quietly listening and soaking up what he said.

"Now, do the pattern again."

I started off doing the pattern and completed it without losing a step or a detail. I was totally immersed in the overlay of knowledge in the simple patterns.

"Good...come with me!"

As we walked away, I concluded that the lesson on the pattern was over.

"Remember when you first started learning the pattern, what did you feel?" He said finally.

"I remember trying to get your approval and attention to make up for the fact that I did not know what I was doing and that I felt uncomfortable."

Bredda Man did not react, but looked at me with an expression of intense, but neutral, focus. I was knocked off balance again. I was not sure how to respond. I felt self-conscious and uncomfortable. I felt his gaze cutting through me like a hot knife through butter.

I searched inside to imagine whether I had said something wrong and fidgeted nervously, feeling really agitated in his unwavering gaze. I was almost in tears and ready to flee my sense of urgent panic, as Bredda Man continued to drive his unrelenting, charged expression through me.

"What do you feel like?" He asked again.

I was relieved to break the anguish of the silence. "I feel really anxious because...."

Before I even finished my thought I realized something important had just been given to me. The immensity of what I realized staggered me. I realized he was testing me again. I realized I was still seeking validation from some familiar expression he would provide. It was no different than doing the form. He had just tested my understanding of the form without telling me we were still under the discipline.

I realized there is never anywhere we are not in the discipline of the pattern. I stood calmly before him and watched in silence and stillness as he drilled the fiery energy of his absolute neutrality into my bones. This time I was really awake. I felt my body shudder and give up any expectation of whether I was right or wrong. I stood totally present in his ancient gaze. Everything became totally still and timeless.

He walked toward me with his hands folded, and I stood, enveloped in a peaceful energy field that was also, somehow, electric.

"Now you can move from the stillness, it is time for you to speak from it."

He pointed to a tree that was nearby. "I want you to speak for this tree from the stillness."

I looked at the tree. It was a small poincianna. I became aware of a rootedness I shared with the tree, extending out in all directions. Then I became acutely aware of my breathing. I focused my intent and spoke, keeping the tone and the speed of my speaking in harmony with the feeling of energized peace Bredda Man had ignited in me.

"Like you tree, I am rooted in the wholeness of Creation. Your branches come from your ancient dark roots to bring your truth into the elements and feed your source. My expressions, my words, movements, feelings and thoughts, also emerge from still, living, rootlike branches. When I remember this root in my branches, I feed my source in Creation."

When I finished I was amazed at how much more clear and alive my words were.

"How do you feel?" He asked me.

"I feel like I am in a new place in myself that was untouched and unknown."

He smiled and spoke calmly, "That is the sign you have done it right…when you feel innocent…it is mysterious. Did you notice the speed and tone of your words?"

I remembered that I spoke slower and more confidently than usual, but I had not consciously chosen to do that. It was the result of my focus on the energy awareness I held. Then I remembered I had felt strange speaking that way. I felt inhibited and almost restrained.

"It's almost as if I was being held back, it felt un-natural," I said.

Bredda Man nodded his head and answered, "Yes…this is not your habitual tone of voice, so it will seem unnatural until you shift your loyalty completely from the old perception of who is speaking. When you are aware of the neutral energy level in your being, you have no agenda. It's the formless aspect of your persona. When you speak with an agenda, and are loyal to your familiar habit, your tone of voice is less powerful, is more agitated and more tense.

"Your intention is weakened every time you speak with an agenda that requires validation. When you speak from the place of responsibility for what you know, your intent is more powerful. Before, you learned to validate your intent through the response of others. So is your natural perception, and expression, of speech. It takes time to adjust and realign…but you will succeed, if you work at it.

"These are the teachings of the four teachers, the Physical, the Imagination, Emotion and Knowing. Now you have been given these teachings—and yet, this is only the first level."

I understood that my Emotions had been tested and that I had learned to remain focused without seeking validation. I was shown how to remain neutral and speak and act from a place of formless knowing. I had learned a lot, but this was only the first level!

We walked through the forest slowly. Bredda Man in front of me, swinging the pendulum. As I watched the pendulum, I started to feel self-conscious. I suddenly realized that I had been learning all along but until now I had not really *understood* what was happening.

When I was around Bredda Man, my body woke up and I felt a charge, like electricity, that emanated from his being, creating a new and unfamiliar posture in my body.

This unprecedented awareness was becoming my frame of reference—my zero balance point. This was the echo and emanation of the zero balance provided by the plumb line of his presence. At first I had felt vulnerable with Bredda Man and I had fought against this vulnerability. But as I learned more, I realized what was beyond the futile labels of discomfort and security I had believed in. I looked toward Bredda Man now and he turned and stood still. He looked at me intently.

I began to experience a deep grief inside me, which frightened me. I was startled by the raw starkness of the feeling. I gasped. Bredda Man was still watching me like a hawk. He waited, and I knew he wanted me to tell him what I had felt. I stammered again. "I… feel such a deep sorrow but I don't understand…. Why?"

Before I could finish, he handed me the pendulum and motioned for me to swing it. I started to swing the stone from one side to the other.

"Do you need to control whether the stone is going to swing back once you start the swing from one side?" he asked.

I answered, "No, the stone will swing back all by itself."

Bredda Man responded, "Aiyihheee!" in a gentle, soft and reassuring tone.

"This is the guardian of the center for the swings of fear and self-doubt. If you get caught by them you can't go straight to the center. Your feelings are just like the stone once they start to swing one way, they are going to come back to the other side without you knowing how, when or why... that is the natural law. Just stay centered and don't try to fix any of the feelings ... let them go just as they are, and watch them without fear ... that is how you will grow straight. Build up the stillness and watch them from that quiet place inside."

Then I went back to the intensity of the sadness I had felt inside, but I chose to focus on watching it instead of reacting to it. Suddenly my awareness shifted dramatically and I felt as if an electric cable was connected to the base of my spine. A wave of energy shook my entire being into a state of awakened vitality.... I was a vibrating energy field whose center was a formless, still energy.

Bredda Man's eyes opened wide and his face radiated a power that was like an intense floodlight coming straight out of the darkness. "So you decided to wake up!"

His words jolted my being as I realized I had never felt so aware or awake in my life before. Every cell in my body was vibrating. I also saw that Bredda Man was awake, too! That was an even more startling realization. I felt that the two of us were alone in the Universe. Everyone else I knew in the world that I usually inhabited was asleep. This was not a judgement on my part. It simply was a certainty! And, I thought, this was also the core of my sadness.

I saw that the Emotional certainty of that sadness and the belief that I was distraught was a trap. In going to the source of the sadness, I established the plumb line's zero balance, and not one of its swings, as the measure of my being. I saw the next level was one of pure detachment. I saw the entire wheel clearly, outside myself, as a protective circle I could use to order and structure the world. I realized I had chosen to enter the center of the wheel.

From that charged, bright center within me, I could look at the certainty of Emotion without any attachment. In realizing this detachment I could not look back, or look for some Emotional validation. I would simply detach my awareness level and observe Emotion without any identification with it whatsoever. This felt strange at first. But each time I managed to stand at the still center, I felt my body energize itself and my posture became more upright. If my resolve wavered for a second, I would fall out of the center.

Bredda Man said, "This is the power of the plumb line, my little bredda! It's pure Consciousness, before we try to grab hold of happiness or throw away sadness and misery. This still place is alive and free John Crow…that is the measure of a person…how long you can stand up in this place and establish your house in this formless, living state. It's one thing to know about this center and another to begin to build a life around it."

I was still vibrating with the power of the charged, living, still point we shared. Bredda Man sensed I was struggling to remain there.

He stood up suddenly and said, "Do you know the form?"

His piercing look threw me back into my center of pure consciousness. I remembered the physical form and how I had thought I knew it. Then he had shown me another level—the application. And then I learned that I had to teach the form to complete my understanding. Now, I realized, this knowing was yet another form. I bowed as an expression of total reverence and to show my understanding of the zero balance within.

"Let us go back now!" That was all he said. It was spoken with neither approval nor judgment, but he had confirmed my understanding.

We walked on, side by side, holding an intensely charged awareness in the space between us. I became more attentive to

Tamah thinks hard but she can't find one part more powerful than the next, so she says, "All the different parts, they are equal."

Maas Chasan say, "Aaaihee! You have a good heart, Tamah, because that is the right answer... the parts of the river look and sound different, but it's still one river. Now there is another thing for you to find out."

Tamah asks, "What is that Maas Chasan?"

Chasan tells her if she wants to find the answer to the problem with the ugly fruit she must learn what the Mountain, the Sun, the Sky, and the Sea know about Water.

Tamah walks all the way back up to the mountaintop and she asks Maas Mountain, "What do you know about Water, Maas Mountain?" Maas Mountain says, "I know the Water as flowing from the cloud to the rain and then from the lake to the cloud." Tamah listens and remembers what Maas Mountain says.

Then she asks Maas Sun what he knows about Water and Maas Sun says, "Water rises up to greet me as mist and bows down before me as rain." Tamah remembers what Maas Sun says.

Tamah follows the river back to the sea and asks Miss Sea what she knows about Water. Miss Sea says, "Water is my body and my heart, always flowing in and out." Tamah remembers what Miss Sea tells her.

Then she asks Miss Sky what she knows about Water. Miss Sky tells her, "Water rides on my gentle breezes and gives shade to my children on the Earth as clouds." Tamah remembers what Miss Sky says.

Then Tamah finds her way back to Maas Chasan.

"Maas Chasan," she says, "I learn everything Maas Mountain and Maas Sun, Miss Sea and Miss Sky know about Water."

Maas Chasan says, "Now there is only one thing more for you to find out before you can go into my cave."

"What is that, Maas Chasan?" She asks.

"You have to tell me what you know about Water!" Miss Tammy realizes she only knows what Mountain, Sun, Sea, and Sky have told her. That is what *they* know about water. She sits down on the bank of the river to think how she will find out what *she* knows.

First thing she does is jump into the Water and she feels cool. Then she drinks the Water and her thirst is quenched. Then she listens to the Water and she feels joy. Then she looks at the Water and she feels peace. It begins to rain, and she smells the Water. She goes under the trees to shelter and she knows quietness.

Tamah thinks she is finished, but then she realizes she should also speak to the Water before she goes back to Maas Chasan.

She asks Water, "Who are you?" and Water answer her straight back, "Who am I?" Tamah remembers what Water says and she goes back to the cave. Maas Chasan stands up in front of the cave and Tamah tells him everything as it happened to her. Then Maas Chasan says to her, "Now you can go into the sacred cave."

Above the cave entrance there is writing, which says, "Know Thy Self." Tamah starts to go into the cave, but Maas Chasan calls after her, "Miss Tammy don't take anything inside the cave with you ... whatever you take with you that's what you will meet inside. "

Tamah leaves everything behind and she goes inside the cave. As soon as she is inside, she realizes she has a small seed from the ugly fruit pushed up under her fingernail. But it is too late. The whole cave fills up fast with the ugly fruit and blocks her way out. She is frightened because the fruit still grows bigger and bigger. She can't move because the ugly fruit is squashing her. All she can do is think. She thinks about what Water said to her.

She remembered she first went far to find out from Sun, Mountain, Sea, and Sky what they knew about Water. Then she went through her own senses, tasting, feeling, hearing, seeing and smelling. Then she heard the same question back when she questioned Water. "Who am I?" Tamah suddenly understands what Water was telling her, and she grabs onto an ugly fruit and eats it. It tastes sweet.

As soon as she eats it, all the rest of the fruit disappears. Tamah comes out of the cave and Maas Chasan asks her if she is finished. Tamah says she is finished, and Maas Chasan stands up in front of the cave's doorway and blocks it so she cannot go back inside. He says she has to go back to her own house and he cannot help her anymore.

Tamah feels hurt but she says "Thank you!" to Maas Chasan. She walks home and feels good because now she knows how to solve her problem.

When she reaches home, she tells everybody they must eat the fruit, and then the trees shrink right down and the problem is gone. Everybody is happy. The fruit tastes sweet and good. It keeps all the people healthy.

Then Tamah meets up with Dagah again and he asks her for a gift. Dagah sits down and Tamah tells him the story about Water and what happened with the ugly fruit. When Dagah stands up, he is a little boy. He and Tamah go out and play all around the forest.

Just as Bredda Man finished the story, a large mongoose ran straight up the path that led to the chicken house. The boys screamed with delight. The chickens started to cluck excitedly behind the wire fence of their run. I ran after the mongoose to make sure he didn't run off with one of the chickens. I followed him into the bush for a while throwing small stones to encourage him to keep going. When I got back to the cabin everyone was gone and so were all the small carvings Bredda Man had made. Only the small scraggly piece of wood remained.

When Bredda Man saw me coming he said, "That one belongs to you." I felt disappointed and tried not to show it.

"It needs some fixin' up. It is Old Man John Crow. You have to finish carve him. But first tell me what you learned from the story."

I tried to remember the story, but my mind was not clear. Bredda Man looked at me and said, "You think your carving is not as pretty as the other ones. That is part of the story, too. Now tell me what you learned before it's time for you to leave."

I knew Bredda Man's tone of voice well enough to realize he was not joking around and he was not going to allow me to sulk, so I put aside my self pity and started to think.

"The people were afraid to eat the fruit and that made it seem worse than it was," I said half-heartedly.

Bredda Man sucked his teeth like it was only half an answer. "What do you do when you swallow something?"

I answered shyly, "It becomes part of me."

Bredda Man smiled and continued, "Yes, the body works on the thing that you swallow to make it into something you can use for nourishment. There is the nourishment for the body and for the heart. When you feel something, whether it is a good feeling or a bad feeling…is a gift…just like the ugly fruit. But unless you work to make the gift into something you can understand, it will drive you this way and that. Imagination is the digestive juice that help to break feelings down so we can nourish the heart."

I remembered the teachings of the plumb line about staying centered, so I waited until I was still inside. Then it came to me, "That's why she swallowed the fruit!"

Now the excitement of the story was already starting to get the better part of my hurt feelings.

"So swallowing the fruit is like accepting things we are not familiar with and don't like, as food to feed our understanding and our knowing, instead of blaming ourselves or someone else…. It's not labeling our feelings as bad … it's staying at the center of the plumb line."

Bredda Man nodded his head and continued as he filled the kettle to make some tea. "That old man Dagah is our fear and Tamah is our innocence. The innocent part of you knows the bush is your home, where everything is sacred ground, where there are no fences and no isolated environments. The ugly fruits are the unnatural traditions. Like when you are taught in school to put your learning into separate boxes. When people take on unnatural traditions and don't understand them, they keep running from or chasing after them all their lives."

I sat up, suddenly struck by the way the story was turning. Bredda Man waited, watching to see if I would find a way through the fence of my thoughts. I went back again to the plumb line teachings … the story was a summary of that entire teaching!

Bredda Man continued, "They say Mongoose guards the Earth and he knows where treasure is buried deep in the bush."

As soon as I heard that I said, "So Mongoose is the part of us that can teach and guide the other parts to understanding. … like the plumb line is the still part."

Bredda Man carefully cleaned out the used coffee cups with a bit of water in a plastic bowl in the sink. Then he said, "We first learn the form physically. We learn to pay attention. We learn to be still. We learn to trust our own Knowing. We learn all these things on a physical level. Then it is time for us to take this knowledge into the realm of Imagination. Here the foundation is our personal stories and myths. Interpreting these becomes our forms and patterns." He looked at me, checking to see if I understood.

He tossed the water from the dishes onto a seedbed outside the window—Bredda Man didn't ever waste anything—and then set the bowl down in the sink again. He dried the cups off and set them down on the counter top. Then he continued, "Mongoose is alive and natural. Mongoose is wild and lives deep in the Earth, yet he can work with people. So that part of us is our Imagination that can teach the other parts to come together. Imagination leads the innocent part to Understand and Know that the natural world is a mirror of who we are. When we take on the name of the wild animals we make our selves the foundation for the knowledge we have gained in the wilderness. We connect to the vitality of the animal spirit to enliven the will in Imagination. It's the same continuum and echo of the still, vital energy of the Formless center."

I was busily trying to figure out why Mongoose took the girl to find the different aspects of Water.

Bredda Man continued, "First thing we have to understand is that we are part of the same Creation. Young or old, human or animal, whether we live clean or bad-minded, it's part of the same river. Plenty of people forget about the elements as a teaching, but all of our knowledge starts with our relationship to them. That is why Mongoose took the girl to know them first, before she can face her fear. The elements, they are in everything. That is the beginning of understanding.

"When we have a solid foundation of knowledge about ourselves, we can face and use our fears. When we don't have a foundation in the natural world, things make no sense and we get frightened easily. If our understanding is not tied to a Physical root we can't remember and use it. That's why people built cathedrals long ago and why people learned patterns of movement and dances to house the teachings. The builders of the cathedrals called themselves Masons, but they also became the builders of character and brotherhood.

"It's like a carpenter who thinks he can use what he has learned from a book. But when he tries to use this knowledge he realizes what he learned there is only half of the whole. It takes practice on the physical level to truly understand. Remember, Water teaches Tamah to overcome her fear. Water changes to meet everything, from mist, to cloud, to rain, to river to sea, all of them are Water. So a challenge is a teacher, a student, and knowledge all at the same time."

"Bredda Man," I said, "both the girl and Water want to know who they are. When Water mirrored the question the girl asked, it's because the essence of Water is fearlessness…Water is not afraid to change. Change is what unites all the different parts of the river. That is why Water is always asking 'who am I?' and echoing whatever it meets."

Bredda Man's eyes lit up, and he smiled a big smile. He snapped his hand like a whip and said, "Go on, John Crow!" excitedly, honoring my answer.

As I followed the trail of the story in my own imagination, I suddenly realized the journey to know Water was first an outside journey, then it was closer… and then it was inside.

I blurted out, "that's how the girl found out she had to eat the fruit of Understanding. Knowing this story is the next step in learning the pattern. Now I am learning it with the story as the foundation. I am learning the pattern from the Imagination instead of the Physical realm. It is harder to see the same pattern I learned in the Physical form. The tracks are less defined than when we did the form Physically. When we start to turn inwards we choose to internalize our search instead of looking for answers outside."

Bredda Man smiled and said, "Instead of tracking the prey of understanding through mud, now we track over rock."

Still smiling, Bredda Man looked at me intensely. I felt a shock, as if something in my awareness had shifted suddenly. Instead of seeing the meaning of the story outside of myself, I was seeing it in relation to my own recent drama. I picked up the carving Bredda Man had given me and realized the carving was an important part of understanding the story.

I wanted to say something to let Bredda Man know that now I understood his gift. I felt foolish. His gift was not meant as a slight or an insult, it was meant to help me to understand the story better. His gift was unfinished because my own involvement was the only thing that would complete it. It required my response and my work. I smiled as this realization dawned on me. The gift had to be made into something that reflected my unity with Creation as well as Bredda Man's knowledge. The carving was something I should use to complete my own understanding and heart. To show Bredda Man that I understood, I started to work on the carving. Bredda Man watched attentively as I began to carve. He smiled and nodded his head.

When the tea was ready, we sat down and drank in silence and then we both went back to our carvings. A couple of hours passed. I sat quietly carving and listening to the far away winds sweeping across the mountaintops—it was my breath.

Then I thought of something and spoke it out loud before I realized what I was saying, "Bredda Man the cave is the darkness of our hearts, which are full of fear when we stop blaming and projecting judgement out onto other people. Fear holds this sword of judgement from inside. When we swallow the fear in that darkness, we understand and can feel our heart's strength is like the river…it responds to whatever carries it… but it's still the same Innocence."

Bredda Man was slow to answer…almost as if he had to come back a long way from the place where his mind and heart were joined to the wood in carving.

Finally, he spoke, "The important thing is to remember the gift hides inside of us, the feelings, whether they are good or bad, they seem like they come from outside. When we hide the fruit of feelings, we don't realize they are a gift, whether ugly or nice. Usually, we either demonize or we praise our feelings. But when we swallow the fruit, we see each feeling as a gift and as a part of the river of our consciousness. This way of accepting what is ours connects us to a deeper reality. We begin to see our inner world and outer world as part of the same expansive space we connect to as we breathe."

Looking satisfied, Bredda Man sat down and went back to his carving. Then he added, almost making light of it, "It's you alone that can make something out of what I give away today."

He looked at me and smiled mischievously and said, "You better go home now before it gets too dark for you to find you way!"

His words struck me to the bone. But his smile told me I had got it! I remembered the lesson of finding gifts in the many feelings that came and went, and I let myself accept this sudden confusion as another gift. It was hard to trust what I knew while the feelings inside flew around like a swarm of angry wasps. I picked up my carving and looked at it proudly. As I reached the door, Bredda Man called after me, "Tomorrow we will go and set the springes and calabans in the forest! Love. Divine Elders. Mother Creation and Father God."

That night I fell asleep, holding close my small carving of Old Man John Crow.

# 10

# The Traps of Belief

THE NEXT MORNING, we set out early with some twine, a machete and a sharp rachet knife to look for places to set the springes in the forest.

Bredda Man said that he wanted me to focus on letting kindness come to everything through my movements. He said, "When you walk, when you talk, when you feel something, when you know something ... feel love and goodness coming out from all your being."

I immediately felt an intense energy stream between us.

"What about the plumb line, then, Bredda Man?" I asked, referring to the balanced, neutral energy I had been practicing.

He replied, "Now give it a conscious spark of kindness."

I walked behind Bredda Man, trying to be aware of my movements. The same intense energy current that I had felt before was there, but now I noticed a subtle sense of detachment in the energy. Then I concentrated on loving kindness and suddenly the energy seemed to become brighter and more nurturing throughout my body.

At first I felt some resistance building inside, which made me nervous, but as I persevered, a reassuring softness emerged. I relaxed and became aware of a great beauty all around me as we moved through the bush. I focused on my

steps tenderly touching the Earth and my body gently dancing with the bushes in a reverent and kind embrace.

We walked a big circle and saw signs of doves and partridges all along the high mountain paths. As we walked, I
was submerged in a peaceful substance that seemed to perme-
ate the forest. Everything responded to my touch with acceptance and welcome.

Then we left the path to gather fallen wood to make the calabans and springs. Bredda Man talked to the forest, "Wake up,
great forest. You see how we come here to clean up and help
keep you healthy and fresh. Yes, that is how we want you to
remember us. We come to help you…that is our work and we
are glad to do it. We come to help you with a good heart. We
come to greet our Holy Land."

As I listened to Bredda Man's kind tone I felt the forest
wake up and become fully aware of our presence.

I felt the forest watching us. The gentle and tender energy
of the exercise I had been doing was suddenly charged with
an intense vibration. Everything in the forest became charged
with the same powerful vibration. Bredda Man looked at me.
His eyes and Body were luminous. "Sit down and listen!" he
said. His voice seemed to come from far away.

We sat together and closed our eyes to listen. I felt myself
catapulted sharply into the forest. I was travelling at great
speed through the vines and branches of the trees, which
seemed to be spun of cobweb-like light. They ran through me
like a bolt of lightning. I knew I was connected to the forest
and all the life there at a very subtle level. After the initial
intensity the energy became softer and found its level, I could
open my heart to the flow of the vibration. I felt an immense
Love for every fiber of the forest's web.

I slowly became aware of my thoughts again and opened
my eyes. Bredda Man was sitting quietly beside me. He pulled

out some rose apples he had picked along the way. The fragrance was heavenly and eating the fleshy crisp yellow fruit reminded me of what I had just experienced.

Bredda Man smiled a huge beaming smile. He turned to me, nodding heartily as he chewed, "Rawtid, maan…. That's how everything in the Holy Land tastes!"

We were very happy and we laughed joyously together.

Bredda Man pulled over some of the dead wood we had collected and set a pile together.

"How are you feeling, John Crow?" he asked softly.

I replied, "I feel good, maan!"

Bredda Man smiled again and said, "Come here make me show you something!"

He drew a circle on the ground and placed four stones in the four directions. "See the West, that one is the Body. See the South, that one is the Dream. See the East, that one is the Heart. See the North, that one is our Intuition and Wisdom." He looked up at me, smiling, and then he placed a flower in the center. It was so simple, clean and beautiful!

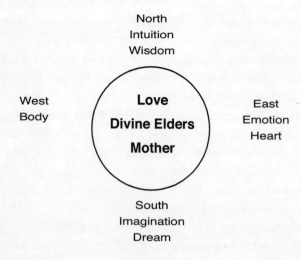

North
Intuition
Wisdom

West
Body

**Love**

**Divine Elders**

**Mother**

East
Emotion
Heart

South
Imagination
Dream

Bredda Man waited a bit and smiled before he spoke again. "When most people speak of love, it is to do with one way of being, with one other person, in one area of Life. Love cannot be isolated in this way. This is the cause of great loneliness and depression in society. True love does not separate us from any of Creation. Love has to emerge from the formless center of our wheel. True love connects us to all Creation. We learn to imagine in loving ways, we learn to be wise in loving ways, we learn to move in loving ways. This is honoring the wholeness of love and the Circle of Human Being."

I nodded my head, thinking about the day and what we had done. I was remembering the exercise Bredda Man had taught me, to bring loving kindness into my energy body and movements. Then something clicked.

I spoke excitedly, "When love comes out of the formless energy it is built on the same true energy of the plumb line rather than any one of the directions, like physical love. Then it can balance the ways we move, our dreams, our feelings and our knowing. The directions are all the ways we can bring love into wholeness."

Bredda Man sat up straight and watched me intently. He pointed to the wheel again. "Seen, John Crow… Love can only be balanced when it works through all of our different natures. Love does not belong to one part of us … that is a misguided ignorance. Love can't be whole if it only involves what we call Heart. That is desire when we talk that way. True Love is at the center of our Human Being and it works through all the four directions equally. That is the true Heart. When the heart works through all the directions, that is the function of the One Heart. You remember when you learned the form and how you thought that you knew it when you had only learned to do the physical movements?"

I remembered all to well.

"It's the same when you could apply the form and then teach it, that's when you really knew it. And that was the beginning of your knowledge, not the end. Love that comes from the conscious center is a form, too. Practising it in one direction is only part of the learning. To know the form of love we become proficient in bringing this force into all our directions from the formless center.

"The Earth, the stones and plants, the way we eat and drink, how we move and dance upon the Earth, how we build our homes and how we manage the wilderness…our physical senses…our practical affairs…our families… that is the West.

"The waters, the animals, and living creatures. The ways we imagine ourselves, our personalities, our dreaming and Imagination, our self image, the ways we identify ourselves and others, our culture … that is the South.

"The fire and the Sun. The ways that we feel and express our feelings and convictions. The ways we validate our sense of knowing. The faith and belief we have in our knowing and self image. Our morality. How and to what we give meaning in our lives. Our heroes and leaders. How we use power and how we are used by it, our nations… that is the East.

"The divine beings. The stars. The sacred laws and scriptures. Our abstract ideas, detachment and clarity. How we use our intuition and knowing to accept our innocence and our vast formless being. The ways that we know Wisdom, and understand things, how we use technology and how we are used by it … that is the North.

"When love is consistent in all the areas in a person's life, we say that person loves truly and is a whole person. Some people say they love the animals and plants, but then they support heroes and leaders who are brutal and mindless. Some people are loving with their families, but in their jobs they are destructive to the Earth and other creatures, or they believe in teachings that enslave other peoples and races.

"The way we can see that love is true, is when it is not separate or isolated from any of these directions. The meaning of the word Love doesn't change from one environment or individual to another…what we have to learn to do is to make our lives a vessel that can hold this meaning consistently."

I stared at the wheel with the flower inside the four stones. The simplicity of his teaching stunned me. I wished school could be this way.

Bredda Man stood up and said gently, "Come nuh, John Crow, help me make up the calabans. Remember to Hold on to the One Heart!" He looked at me to see that I knew he was referring to the exercise of letting goodness come through my movements. I nodded and he understood.

Bredda Man cleaned several long thin half-dried saplings and gave them to me to notch and cut into pieces for the springes. I whittled out enough for five springes, five crooks and support posts, five trigger twigs and five lengths of twine.

Then he cut the saplings for the calabans and handed me the first four for the bases. I strapped these together to form a neat square. I also notched and cut the two holding poles in half sections, so they would fit together snugly.

The whole time I was working I felt perfectly at peace with the forest. My work was a celebration of the forest and showed our respect for her.

I tied the twine onto the calaban bases, from each corner so the twine formed an "X" through the center of each square base that could be lifted up in the center to form a pyramid of twine. Then we laid down the cut saplings log cabin style, until we got to the where the twine crossed where we slid smaller and smaller twigs in, until the whole thing was really tight and sturdy.

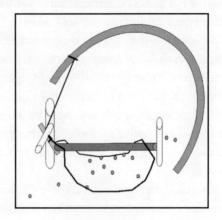

Springe

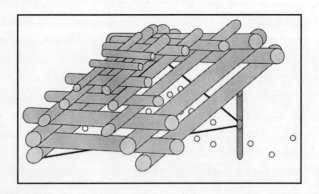

Calaban

We finished the calabans by rubbing them with some green leaves and dirt to make them blend into the forest.

Bredda Man said, "When we make something without love, we charge it with separateness and fear. All the forest feels this separation. Some people have much technology when they hunt but there is no love in it. After eating any food that is killed without love the belly is full but the soul remains hungry. To feed on the Holy Land we must first awaken her. Then the food we eat will nurture many generations."

Just then a little banana quit flew onto a branch right above Bredda Man's head. Banana quits are usually elusive and shy little birds. But she was chirping away, looking quite unconcerned about us. Bredda Man slowly lifted his hand up to the branch. The little bird sat quietly and when Bredda Man touched her feet with his fingers she hopped onto his hand. Looking like a little chick in its mother's care, the little bird perched contentedly on his hand.

Bredda Man hummed quietly, and I felt the same intense love again drawn from my being. The little bird hopped onto my shoulder and chirped for a while. I knew she was telling us her story and how she was glad we were here, caring for the Earth and remembering Love. Then she flew off into the bush.

Bredda Man spoke, "When we awaken the Holy Land, everything is a blessing. Every thing will come to us in a holy way."

I got a strange feeling as we walked back to the circle that we scouted out for our traps. "Then how could we be in the Holy Land and intent on killing?" I asked myself.

I was focusing on the exercise of channelling love, but this question bothered me. Bredda Man stopped and drew the circle on the ground again. "John Crow, remember the circle. We are all part of this circle. He pointed to the West and said this is the place of the Elements and the plants. He put the Animals in the South. He put Humans in the East and in the North he said there was the Spirit world. In the middle he said there was the One Heart.

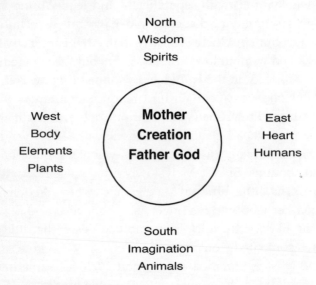

North
Wisdom
Spirits

West
Body
Elements
Plants

**Mother
Creation
Father God**

East
Heart
Humans

South
Imagination
Animals

"We are all part of the circle in life and in death. How we live and die— not whether we live or die—is what this work is about. The animals have been here longer than we have and they have promised to keep the sacred Circle of Life alive by showing us that love is stronger than death. The animals are all warriors of the spirit in this way, John Crow. They give us their bodies in love so we can live. It is only when we accept their gifts with love, honor and respect that their gift is complete.

"Everything is food. The entire body of the Earth is made up of the remains of our ancestors, dead animals and dead plants. We are eating the recycled bodies and awareness of generations. When we choose to kill with reverence for the gifts and sacrifices of another being, we are not taking we are giving something back. When we choose to make love our true habit, then we become food for the highest spirit within the Earth. This spirit renews the Earth and all the creatures upon it when we human beings offer our limitations and fears as food for love and wholeness. Then we are open and generous to the whole of Creation. There is humility in this balancing of giving and taking. When we take without respect for the sacrifices of the animals or plants we feed carelessness and fear.

"We learn first by offering our pains and fears to our energy awareness and loving kindness. Then we feed the energy awareness. When we offer the sacrifice of our energy awareness to love we awaken the spirit of the Holy Land within all Creation. That Great Spirit that dwells within the Earth is awakened. The power of awakening the Holy Land in our food makes it nourishing for seven generations.

"These warriors, John Crow, these little children from the Earth are fearless and true. That is why they give their lives to us...to help us to remember True Love, my little bredda. Yes, maan...it's to remember True Love and remember how to awaken the Holy Land. Even if we only awaken Her one time...that one time will change our Heart for ever!"

I understood immediately the meaning of what Bredda Man said.

We walked silently into the forest to set our traps. Each time we set a trap, we charged the area with an atmosphere of kindness and respect for the forest's children who would choose to become part of our lives as food.

"Love, we love our brothers and sisters, who are free and yet choose to honor us in this way. Their gifts help us to remember that we, too, give our bodies to feed a greater purpose. Every time we bring our Lives into harmony with the Wisdom teachings and the Formless Heart of the plumb line, we give our bodies to feed the subtle powers within."

When Bredda Man said this I realized a basic truth. In almost everything we do, we take another being's life so that we can live. Even when we just walk, we kill hundreds of small insects and tiny organisms underfoot.

The chickens we buy in the supermarkets did not live lives that were respected. The people who put them into small cages and fed them steroids and hormones to make a profit did not care for their gifts.

My life was no different when I lived my life asleep to the meaning of Creation. I too was in a cage and was fed unhealthy food for someone else's profit.

Here in the forest I had a chance to honor the spirit of freedom by choosing to love all Creation. I thought about living my whole life this way, respectful of all the sacrifices made to keep me alive. My choice to wake up and live with reverence for Creation's gifts to me would give meaning to my life. Then, finally, my own death would be the culmination of this Knowledge and a gift that was a respectful appreciation of all Creation.

Before we left the forest I spoke my gratitude to the forest. "I learned a lot from you today great forest. My heart is full of goodness and thanks for what you have shown us."

# 11

# The Gift of Death

EARLY ONE MORNING, before the Sun was up, we went into the mountains to check the springes and the line of calabans. I gathered some twine and the rachet knife and our sling shots and we set off in the dark. We reached the mountain pond just as the first rays of the Sun came over the horizon.

Bredda Man sat still, looking down the mountain slope toward the Sun. He closed his eyes and motioned for me to sit with him. He spoke, "I maan give this body to thee, Great Queen, Mother Creation, Mother Earth, Mother Elements. For this body belongs to thee and I maan keep it healthy to help me to learn and grow. I maan can love the way you love Creation. I take thy heart into my chest and I shall keep it with me this day shining bright like a star, in the universe of my body. Mother and Queen hear me and hold me close."

As he spoke the whole hillside seemed to listen. Bredda Man reached out with both hands toward the Sun as if he was taking it and pulling it into himself. He patted it into his body. Then he held his hands on his chest as if he was holding the Sun inside his heart.

We watched in silence as the Sun rose. I felt a burning in my heart and tears started to stream down my face. I didn't know why I cried, but tears of joy and sadness, peace and pain came to me as I watched Bredda Man blessing and greeting the day.

Then Bredda Man taught me the Sun ritual. He told me first to imagine I was breathing the Sun into my Body through my open hands in a gesture of blessing. And then, when I was breathing out, I was sending my breath into the heart of the Sun. We did the ritual together until the Sun had fully risen. He told me exchanging energy with the Sun this way was a very healthful thing to do.

Bredda Man asked me to draw the circle with the four directions and tell him what I remembered. I marked the four directions in the Earth where we sat. He watched me intently as my hand moved reverently around the circle. When I told him all I remembered of the directions and their meanings, he smiled and nodded his head.

Then we went into the bush to check the springes. Bredda Man was watching me carefully as we moved through the bush. I remembered the exercise of keeping the Sun in my heart and letting it shine love through my movements. Before, I had moved with love animating my body. Now I was also bringing my intuition into the expression of this love. I thought about the Circle and knew that Bredda Man was going to teach me how to show my spirit next!

Just then we came to the first calaban. There were feathers all around it, but nothing inside. Bredda Man stooped down and smiled. "Our bredda, the mongoose, took our pea dove for his children." I laughed. Bredda Man turned the calaban over so it would weather until we came back again.

When we saw the next calaban there was a definite presence around it. As we got closer, the bird that was caught inside panicked and feathers flew about.

I was excited and dashed toward the calaban, frightening the dove even more.

Bredda Man called out sharply to me, "John Crow!" I stopped in my tracks. I was tingling with nervous excitement.

Bredda Man stood still and called me firmly back. As I retreated toward him, the bird quieted down.

Bredda Man put his hand on my shoulder and said quietly, "Is not easy for their hearts to receive what we feel. Now is the time for you to know love in your movements!"

I realized at once what he was saying.

"Act like a man who is aware of being given a great honor. Is not every day one of our breddren give us the gift of their life. Make this gift sacred, John Crow!"

I remembered what it meant to receive their sacrifice. This is the moment I had been practicing for. I was so excited about catching something in the calaban that I had forgotten completely about the loving gift I was being honored with. Instead, I had rushed in on the surge of impulsive energy.

As I stood silently beside Bredda Man and focused on my radiant heart exercise, I immediately was able to feel the dove's powerful presence and her receptivity to us. I felt an immense and loving energy from the dove, accepting us as the recipients of her gift. It was as if we were being chosen, instead of the dove being our trapped and helpless victim.

My impulsive, superhero agitation again tried to surface, but I remembered about feeding the elders inside of me and I fed it immediately to the focus of my heart. The more I entered into my open, silent heart space and fed my agitation to my Emotions and Imagination, the more my agitation subsided.

I felt ashamed to have rushed in so irreverently while this being had come to fulfill a great promise and to honor us with her life. My body trembled as I met the dove's eyes. I felt Bredda Man's hands gently squeeze my shoulder.

"Move with love to accept you sister gift!"

I was full of awe as I slowly approached the calaban. The air was infused with a strange and beautiful light. Each step forward required a great effort of will. I felt as if I was being measured by the forest, the animals, and every elder in Creation. As I moved toward her, the dove held me with a look of immense sweetness. I felt I was in the presence of a great being.

This time she did not flap about in panic but calmly walked around inside the calaban. I opened it and gently lifted her out. I felt her warm head resting on my fingers. Her heart beat very fast in the shallow cup of my hands. When Bredda Man approached, I handed him the dove. He took the dove and held her tenderly against his chest. The dove was now quiet and very calm. Bredda Man looked at me and I felt a great love between us all as we stood in the forest.

Bredda Man stroked the dove. He hummed softly—in the same way as when he had moved the wasp nest. Then, with a sudden, strong movement, he broke the dove's neck. He stood upright and turned slowly around, offering the bird's body to the four directions, holding it up and spreading out the wings.

The eerie light still surrounded us. Staying firmly in my heart exercise, I felt a surge of energy move through the forest. My hair stood on end.

Bredda Man pulled some of the feathers from the dove's breast and offered them to the four directions. They floated on a gentle breeze to the forest floor. It was very quiet. We stood still, listening. The crickets and all the animals were silent. The silence lasted for a few more seconds and then gradually the forest noises started up again.

Bredda Man handed me the dove and showed me how to tie it to my belt by threading twine through the beak. Then he sprinkled some corn and tobacco in the four directions and we moved on to the next trap. There were three more birds caught in three of the springes, but they were already dead. Each time we took a bird Bredda Man sprinkled some corn and tobacco in a circle marking the four directions and offered their bodies to the elements and to our hearts.

We turned over all the calabans and cut the fishing line off the saplings on the springes before we left the forest.

Walking home with our four doves, I felt Bredda Man continue to watch me carefully. This was no mere hunting adventure. I was being initiated into an ancient circle of commitment between humanity, the animals and the great power we know with every cell of our being.

Bredda Man had reminded me to see beyond my habitual, impulsive agitation. When I opened my heart and truly saw what was happening between the dove and myself, I had accepted the invitation to join this ancient community of guardians. In learning how to accept the gift of death I had to give up being in control. I had to give up my isolation from the rest of Creation.

When we got back to the cabin, Bredda Man gave the birds to me to clean and pluck. He told me that we should keep the tail and wing feathers.

I felt a strange tension as I sat down to pluck the birds. I remembered Bredda Man's instructions to hold the Sun inside my Heart. As soon as I imagined this, I felt calm and peaceful again. I felt their gift was honored because of my respect for them and that I had become worthy of their gifts. I felt as if the birds were passing their strength on to me because I was being reverent and loving. Then I understood what Bredda Man meant when he said that awakening the Holy Land in our food makes it nourishing for seven generations.

I carefully put aside the wing and tail feathers. I washed the birds off in an old enamel pan. I washed the other feathers, too, and gathered them up with some mud and made them into a big mound. Then I cleaned out the insides and offered them to the four directions, to Mother Creation, and to Father

God. I placed the insides at the base of a tree facing the Sun for the John Crows. And, finally, I sang quietly the prayer Bredda Man had taught me.

"Just like you, I will be honored in my passing into a greater world than the familiar one I have known and loved so long. Just like you, my knowledge and being will feed this greater presence and will become part of a greater circle. Just like you, I will choose this sacrifice with great love and great respect. Just like you feel my gratitude and respect, now I, too, will feel the gratitude and respect of the great presence I make my sacrifice to."

Bredda Man had already started a fire. We roasted the birds together with a breadfruit and some corn.

As we ate our feast, a huge flock of pea doves flew overhead, so close we could hear their wings beating. They flew around us as if they were honoring us for the care and appreciation we had shown their family.

Bredda Man nodded his head, "One Love brethren, One Love."

# 12

# Dancing Inside the Traps of Belief

BREDDA MAN SAID he would be busy with his carving and healing work in the country for a while. He told me to look for him at the next full moon.

Almost the whole month had gone by. One morning I was at the market with my mom. A politician was talking on the radio about how he wanted to be everyone's champion. He said the same things over and over, loudly and with great enthusiasm, so people would remember his words. Something about what he said bothered me. I was busy trying to figure out why, when I suddenly spotted the old man who sold coconuts. He smiled and nodded at me as I passed by. I knew immediately that his smile was a quiet communication that Bredda Man was back. I waved to him and smiled to acknowledge his message. As soon as I got home and helped put the groceries away, I set off straightaway down the hill to Bredda Man's house.

Bredda Man was mending fences and working in his garden. He greeted me warmly and handed me a machete, pointing to the overgrown grass around the house.

I set to work chopping the tall grass, stopping to sharpen the machete every now and again with a small, worn hand file. As I worked I could hear Bredda Man singing softly. After a few hours I was tired, sweating, and hungry.

Luckily, Bredda Man said it was time to stop working and make something to eat. He asked me to get the fire started while he set up the outside cooking pan.

I knew how to make a fire without matches because I had watched Bredda Man do it many times. I cut some kindling and used some of the burnt cotton he kept in his old biscuit tin. The wood was not dry, so there was a lot of smoke. But that was good because the mosquitoes were plentiful.

In the meantime, Bredda Man had brought out salt fish, yam, green banana and ackee. First, he put the salt fish in the pot to boil while I washed off the sticky sap from the yam and the green banana. I peeled them and cut the yam into thin slices so it would cook faster. The skins went to the compost. Then I prepared the ackee while Bredda Man made "flabbas," or "bullets," (big, flat, flour dumplings that are one of Jamaica's staple foods). We drew some fresh water and put the yam and green banana into the pot with the cooked salt fish. The ackee was added last. In Jamaica we call this pot "dasheen," meaning whatever we have we "dash into" the pot. Finally, Bredda Man added pimento and some spices that he had collected in the bush.

The food tasted delicious. Bredda Man always ate less than I did because he chewed each mouthful about fifty times. He joked and said that diet worked the best! When I remembered to chew my food as well as Bredda man, I didn't eat so much and it always tasted better, too.

I told Bredda Man about the politician I heard speaking on the radio.

Bredda Man was silent. When he responded, it was with a question, "If the animals want to give us their gifts, why do we have to trap them?"

I was shocked. I wasn't prepared for his question and fumbled around for an answer. I finally said, "I don't know."

"Plenty people say they want to learn things, you know, John Crow. But there are those among us who believe learning is a struggle and that is what makes it hard to teach us... we believe we learn this way, struggling and fighting. Then we believe we are important, and the wise have a duty to spend time with us and to teach us even though we are unable to learn and we fight against our knowing. Unless we take time to build an environment where wisdom can become food inside our heart, we will never understand our true gifts.

"What did you understand when you stood back and saw the bird in the trap?"

I remembered feeling tense and that my excitement was out of control. I answered, "I was not prepared to accept the gift of Creation in the trap."

"What made you feel respect and open your heart to the gift of the bird?"

I felt a little shy and said softly, "I trust what you say."

Bredda Man smiled and said, "Aaaaih! So you understand. That is how we feed the elders, by building a space, a living relationship where trust can teach us how to get nourishment from our wisdom.

"The heart is the center of all learning, John Crow. Remember how we pray and what we offer to the Queen and her elements?"

As I thought about what Bredda Man said I felt the excitement that always heralded an understanding and shift inside, like the winds and clouds gathering before the rain falls. "Yes, we say we give our bodies to the Queen and the elements in One Love."

Bredda Man nodded slowly and seriously, "That is the gift of the wise, John Crow, like the birds and the animals give their whole being, the wise give their essence to Creation. That is the true gift of human being.

"Remember the river, John Crow. The waterfall gives itself to Creation one way. The pool in another way. The rapids in yet another way. Each of these are the ways of the river. This is how it is within us also. We give with our body, with our imagination, with our emotions, and also with our wisdom. Each of these are different ways of giving, but they are all human.

We say we have free will, but we do not believe we can create Heaven here on Earth, which is the ultimate freedom. This is the freedom that was outlined by the elders as the Garden of Eden, the template of the true human being. In this primal environment, every being communicated with every other being. Every being touched and was touched by every other being—God, the angels, humans, animals, plants, everything. The template outlined the different aspects of the human river, each working in a unique way in a living relationship with the other parts of human being. The animal part was our self image and magnetism. The angelic part was our emotions. The divine part was an allegory for our essential wisdom.

"This primal way of being is the earliest map of humanity. It is all about giving ourselves completely to this way of being called Creation. This way of being is who we are, it is not what we try to be or want to be! Only the wise give themselves completely as food to this way of being. Most of us believe the physical world is the only one we must feed and make sacrifices to in order to survive. We feed only the physical form from morning till night. We boast about our hard work and believe we are not lazy at all. When it comes time to feed the other parts, we have no energy left. Then we take ganja or rum for our hard working body to relax. And that is slavery because rum and ganja pollute everything by creating craving and separation instead of embracing wholeness. The imagination, and the emotional and the wise parts need food and sacrifice, too. How can we say we are making offerings, when it's not love or wholeness that is inside of us, but some substance that isolates us from wholeness and truth?

"The ignorant among us fight against being food to the deeper part of us, to the ancient wholeness we know as the Garden. Yet still, the ignorant must feed somebody or something. It's only the wise who can choose to step back and receive the gift of Creation without fear of being food. That is the warrior's strength! What would have happened if you didn't listen and you rushed in to grab the bird?"

I was silent. I thought about it and said I realized I would have never known the beauty of the heart's seeing.

Bredda Man nodded his approval and continued. "Seen, John Crow," he said, acknowledging my sincere attention.

"So when you move from impulsive habit … to approach the wise teacher within … do you make it easier or harder for you to appreciate wisdom?

I knew the answer, "Of course, it is harder for me to honor wisdom if I am agitated."

"Stand up here, make me show you something, John Crow."

Then Bredda Man asked me to walk forward and tell him what I was doing in every detail as I walked. I felt awkward and disoriented as I tried to focus on my walking. It was hard to walk at my normal pace and report exactly every movement and shift in weight that occurred. I stopped and shrugged my shoulders in defeat. "I can't do it, Bredda Man, it's not possible."

He laughed and said, "So, you see, that is the way we have learned in our generation, and it's the same way every generation has learned. The way we talk, the way we move is learned from society. We believe we are in harmony with the culture around us when we speak and move in the ways we learned. But this way may not be in harmony with our own knowing and our ability to communicate our knowing clearly. We have to face the fear of going against what we learned in order to reclaim our heart as the center of our world. When we first start to examine the way we speak and move we meet the guardian duppies (spirit forms)."

Bredda Man stood beside me. "Close your eyes. The first thing is to slow down and breathe. Now watch your breathing …and when you hear your thoughts call out for you to follow them, just stay in one place. Stay focused…watch the breath come and go, like the sea. Watch the breath rise up and fall down.…Watch the breath vanish like the day into the night. Then watch the breath come out of stillness like the Sun rising up each day to bring life to the world. Say to yourself, 'I am breathing and I can't leave to follow my thoughts and impulses.' Tell them you are guarding the fire inside for your elders and make them go on without you.

"Let the thoughts go. Feel the light of the inner fire of still-ness. In and between each of your breaths, go deeper into this stillness and let the fire grow brighter. Make the breaths rise and fall from the fire energy of awareness inside. Be aware of your awareness as a glowing fiery mass before it becomes pain or pleasure, images or impulses, one feeling or another, or one teaching or another. Just stay in the energy awareness. If you feel pain, see it as energy instead of pain. Let your thoughts go. Stay focused on the breath inside and feel the radiant fire of peace and stillness grow as you focus in and between each breath. Each breath emanates from and returns to this radiance. Watching the breath this way is what we call Keeping the Elders' Fire."

I imagined the in-breath as the moment before dawn. The space between the in-breath and the out-breath became the radiant Sun. I imagined the out-breath to be the daylight fading through sunset into a night sky. Then the space between these breaths became the fully resplendent Sun again. I watched my breath, and I started to feel a stillness emerging from within the space between each breath.

Bredda Man asked me to open my eyes and describe what I felt.

I realized I was still in a state of deep quiet. I tried to think which words to use, and the only one that came to mind was "peace." I stammered, struggling to say it convincingly. I finally managed to say it, but it did not feel the same as when I was inside the stillness. When I started to explain this to Bredda Man I found I had completely lost touch with the stillness as soon as I started to speak.

He smiled and said, "Now close your eyes and go back to keep the fire again."

As soon as I closed my eyes the brightness returned. I focused on my breath again. I watched as each calm breath gently fanned the brightness into golden flames.

Bredda Man spoke again, "Open your eyes, John Crow."

This time, when I opened my eyes everything had a golden glow around it. I looked around in awe, remembering the golden flames I had seen inside.

"Now, when you tell me what you see and feel, make a tone in your voice that connects you to what you see and feel inside."

My mind moved like some ancient behemoth, searching for a way to express what I saw and felt inside. I started to speak slowly and in a soft, warm tone. As I spoke, I felt a connection to the fire inside again.

"I saw the fire, Bredda Man... and I felt it as I spoke."

Bredda Man smiled broadly and nodded his head.

He waited awhile and then he asked gently, "So what happened to the fire after you finished speaking this time?"

"I felt a deep warmth coming from here," I said, pointing to my chest.

He smiled brightly. "Aiyihee! That is fantastic, my little bredda. Now, close your eyes again!"

His voice carried me deeper inside. It was as if I had slipped into a deep pool of bright, clean water. I observed my breath again, rising and falling, moving through me like some invisible ocean tide. Fire suddenly sparked through my body in tiny explosions. I shuddered as it surged up my body and my spine involuntarily stretched and straightened itself.

Then Bredda Man spoke again, "Open your eyes! Now get up and move in a way that keeps you connected to the Elders' Fire."

I was still. I knew the only movement that would be truthful to the way I felt was to dance joyously.

"Walk so I can see your fire!" Bredda Man shouted. His voice was an arrow of energy that pierced my heart.

I opened my eyes and walked. My heart fire blazed in every step I took.

"Now ... how do you feel when you walk?"

I realized I had made the fire inside grow brighter. "I feel light and strong, Bredda Man."

He smiled and said, "Now that is the way to connect and stay rooted to the Earth. Don't let anybody else's fire draw you away from keeping the Elders' Fire, yaaah! Now walk and tell me exactly what is going on and use what you've learned to tell me. Everything is the dance, maan ... everything is the dance ... so, dance!"

I was amazed at how easy it was to report what I was doing as I walked from a sense of connection to that fire inside.

"I am lifting my heel off the ground. My toes are leaving the ground. My foot is going forward. My heel is touching the ground. My toes are touching the ground. My weight is going forward."

The tone and rhythm of my voice echoed the fire I felt inside. It matched the movements of my body perfectly. Bredda Man was right, everything was a part of that dance. I only had to connect with it by finding a rhythm that was my own. I felt as if my whole being was aligned to a magnetic north deep inside. My spine was a plumb line of fire that echoed the Queen's magnetic power.

Bredda Man danced alongside me. Back and forth we went in the grass, speaking softly to the Heavens and the Earth as we tended the Fire of the Elders. I realized I was simply one little part of the dance of the Queen—just another tiny vibration— but I was content. This knowing was a feast for my spirit fire.

When we finished dancing, Bredda Man made some tea and we sat down together.

He began, "The elders, our inherent wisdom, live and feed on the traps of belief. These are the ways we behave, how we move and speak. The elders need the hunter to make these beliefs into nourishment. The calaban, the elder and the hunter are all parts of the Formless Heart.

"Wisdom has an outer husk and an inner seed. The inner seed is formless and lives in everything. When we build a trap for wisdom we are creating an environment where the outer husk can become food. When we take in the food we own the gift of wisdom as part of us.

"To build the trap and to hunt wisdom takes skill and caring. This is a deep caring to serve and honor the elders."

Bredda Man stopped and looked at me. I was listening carefully. I felt wide awake. But then, once again, Bredda Man asked a question that caught me completely off guard.

"What does the act of killing do?" He asked.

Bredda Man had taught me to stay focused with the Plumb Line exercise, which meant remaining neutral and listening without judging, either outwardly or inwardly. I had learned that I did not need to understand right away. I did not need to demonize myself with judgment, thinking "I am stupid," nor did I need to judge Bredda Man by indulging in confusion. In this way I could make contact with the fear behind my judgments. Usually this meant I feared being ridiculed or being vulnerable. Then I would swallow the fear and feel it as energy. When I listened this way, without letting the energy I felt be named as fear, I felt connected to Bredda Man and the intention behind his words. It would sometimes take months for me to understand completely what he had said.

Bredda Man saw that I was getting agitated. He waited patiently. My thoughts became all jumbled up, but finally I managed to see a clear path, "It changes a way of knowing the world."

Bredda Man nodded his head seriously and went on. "The outer form of wisdom changes so it can become food and transform us from within. The inner form of wisdom does not change or die. It is always whole. It takes a different kind of hunter to find food from this inner level of wisdom."

He looked at me again and asked, "When the body get wounded or bruised and it feels pain…does the pain have any purpose?"

I thought for a while and replied, "Yes, it reminds us to be careful of the sore area so it can heal faster.

Bredda Man continued, "So pain is designed to teach us to be conscious." He smiled. His eyes were intense and bright as he paused.

"Where comes the deep formless wisdom that creates all the different forms to learn from?"

I was not sure, so I answered with an assumption I thought was obvious. "It must be loving."

He smiled again and nodded his head. "It's a very deep caring, little bredda. The intention of this caring is to know beyond our outer skin. Otherwise, when we were wounded or bruised, we would attack our sore parts and wounds as enemies, believing they were endangering our well being."

I laughed at how ridiculous this idea seemed.

Bredda Man continued, "So when we accept pain in our body as a teacher we learn about carefulness, and we can move beyond the physical to a more conscious, mindful awareness."

I nodded, quietly thinking about all this.

The Formless Heart places the seeds of wisdom inside our imagination, our emotions and mind to be awakened. The outer husk of these seeds are felt as judgments and painful wounds. The inner seeds are fears and concepts that hide the vastness of the Formless Heart until we own these fears. Then we can awaken the Formless Heart hidden within them. Just like the physical body, our wounds and judgments are gifts to help us locate and remember where our healing needs to be focused.

Then Bredda Man startled me again with another question.

"Have you ever called anyone a bad name?"

Whenever I was getting comfortable with the subtle aspects of what I understood, Bredda Man had a way of shocking me into a different mode.

"Yes!" I replied.

"What did you really do?"

I was a little confused because I never thought about this before. Then I realized what the process was. I said, "I observed something a person identified with—something that had meaning to him—and I used it to hurt his feelings."

Bredda Man nodded and said, "That is what everyone does. Behind every insult is an observation. "

"What happened when you did that?" he asked, looking at me innocently.

I replied, "He got hurt and upset."

He smiled and nodded. "So what if the whole world knew pain as our teacher and friend?"

I laughed nervously when I imagined people saying, "thank you!" to me for upsetting them.

"How would you react if people said things to show you where your sore spots are?" I understood what he was saying now.

I answered, "I would be respectful and grateful for the chance to learn to be careful and become more aware."

"And how would you point things out to others, then, if you really knew this?"

I chuckled again. "I would be a lot more observant and careful, and respectful, too."

Then I realized something else. I would get caught in other people's ups and downs as much.

Bredda Man went on. "Yes, maan…when we are attached to the outer husk or form of wisdom, we can't understand its inner purpose… like the body's pain, if we bump into someone, is to remind us to be careful and remember where our care needs to be focused to help our wound to heal. The intention of the Formless Heart is to move us to a more conscious knowledge using all our senses and faculties. When we react to others with judgment, is like attacking the part of our body that is hurt or wounded."

He turned to me and shouted, "You are an old shriveled up lime tree."

I was confused.

Bredda Man laughed and shook his head.

"You see, that does not mean anything to you because the Formless heart did not plant that seed for you to tend and grow...that seed is not inside you waiting for healing. Wherever there is a seed of wisdom that we have not awakened yet, our pain and judgment will tell us where it rests. Now if I say something that hurt your feelings you would wonder what happen. You would start thinking whether you did something to upset me and all kind of things because it bothers you. Now if you take the thing that bothers you and treat it like the pain you feel when you have a wound or a sore bruise, what would you do?"

I replied, "I would realize that person could see my sore spot and it was not healed yet. I would recognize the pain as a pointing out where a seed of wisdom rested and required my work to awaken it. I would have to take better care of it to make sure it was healed."

Bredda Man laughed.

I laughed, too, thinking how this sounded ridiculous.

"Nobody does this, Bredda Man ... we fight if people call us names that touch our sore spots and point out where our seeds of wisdom are planted."

Bredda Man looked at me seriously and continued.

"When we see from the elder's perception, the wound is the outer form of wisdom. The outer form is a way to get our attention focused ... so we move inward. Our inner wisdom is always inside these forms we get attached to, in order for us to see and understand. Every wound, every sickness, every hurt we feel is the outer form of a seed of wisdom.

"When we understand we connect to the inner seed, the essence of our wisdom. Understanding requires will, little bredda ... conscious will. Unless we are steady when we build these traps to contain the elders' gift of perception and nourishment, we cannot understand how this works.

"Most people are not hunters, John Crow. Most of us feed a passive way of relating to the seeds of wisdom. The way we do this is by becoming the trap of belief. We become the trap of belief instead of the hunter who builds it. We believe we have to fight against nature. We fight against our natural instincts to succeed. We fight crime. We fight disease. This way of being is like when you rushed in without respect for the teacher inside you.

"That is the calaban of belief we build inside ourselves to reflect what we believe society requires of us. The calaban, the hunter and the elder's wisdom are all a part of our circle of knowing. When we identify with the hunter we believe wisdom is inside a trap we built. Our wisdom's power may appear to be trapped by our habits. This is an illusion. Our wisdom is married to our habits. When we learn to approach our wisdom with care and respect we will always be nourished in a deep way.

"Make me hear you speak for the elder that was in the calaban, John Crow."

I struggled to gather my awareness and make the leap into applying my understanding. I finally spoke.

"Like you wise elder, a part of me is patient and accepting of my habitual impulsiveness and agitation. This part is nourished when my impatience is examined and restrained to reveal the fear behind it. When I know and accept the fears that drive me to impulsive and careless behavior, I too am free like you, to give wholly of myself. I feel this wholeness when I take the time to speak for Creation. I feel stronger when I speak carefully and mindfully. I feel like I am the power of the Sun when I honor my heart in these careful ways. My wisdom is like the Sun and gives the sore, weak parts of myself the light they need so that they will grow toward truth."

Bredda Man smiled and nodded his head slowly.

Then he continued, "Each generation sees the outer form of wisdom in a different way. But the elders are an expression of the formless essence of wisdom. So when we learn to see through their eyes we have a greater perspective. The elders use each generation's beliefs as tools to teach us. Our habits and conditioning are food for the elders. The wise use the beliefs of each generation to complete their work. Understanding requires will, little bredda... conscious will. This is the work we do of speaking for Creation. It is the beginning of your healing work.

"It's like where we walk for one day... the grass grows back. When we walk the same way every day, soon there is a path. A path is like a belief we have as one person. When enough people believe in the same things they all use a similar path, and this path becomes a road. This is like our culture. Then some people will try to act differently. But unless they know where the road comes from—and where it is going— they, too, travel as blindly as everybody else. It takes a lot of wisdom to know how to travel on the road of culture without being controlled by it and without losing ourselves.

"Many people learn to observe and overcome their impulses but then remain attached to the physical form. These people can convince themselves into believing right is wrong and black is white. This is another form of outer wisdom that no longer has a hold over us any longer when we understand.

"When politicians and Obeah men try to manipulate people is no different. Remember when I called you a lime tree?"

I laughed and nodded my head.

"Now if I try to build up a movement based on reaching people who look like lime trees, I would not be very popular. The first thing a politician or Obeah man has to know is what people want and fear. Is who give that power to him?"

I replied cautiously, "If we are afraid or desire things then it is we who give that opportunity to him."

"Aaaih!" Bredda Man shouted. "And if we don't take care to understand where our wounds and bruises are and heal them, and if somebody bumps into them and hurts us, then whose fault is it?"

I was not sure, and I said I thought it could be either one.

"If it happens twice, and then three times, whose fault is it?"

"Then, it's the person who has the bruise who is to blame."

Bredda Man laughed. He sighed and then continued.

"Yes, little bredda, is true, but not many of us take the time and care to know where our weakness is and how we let it rule us. If we need praise to feel like doing something good for our self, then it is easy for somebody to control us with praise. If we do bad things when we feel we are no good, then powerful people who want us to do bad things will make sure we feel bad about our self so we can do things for them."

Bredda Man got up and went inside to put the kettle on again. I followed him and sat down. He offered me some hard dough bread and butter.

After he chewed on his bread for a while and sipped his tea, he said thoughtfully, "Now is time for you to go down into the caves to call a duppy!"

Bredda Man said it, matter-of-fact, like it was something everybody did. But I suddenly felt dizzy and started to fidget nervously.

Trying not to burst into laughter, Bredda Man just smiled and said calmly, "You must practice every day dancing and speaking to keep the Elders' Fire. In two weeks time, we can go to the cave for you to call a duppy."

# 13

# Calling the Duppy

THE TIME PASSED QUICKLY. I practiced my dancing and speaking every day to keep the Elders' Fire alive. Some days it seemed as if there was a visible glow around me.

Finally, one Saturday afternoon I set off with Bredda Man to a special cave in the mountains where I would try to call a duppy.

After two hours of hard climbing, we stopped to rest on a rocky outcrop. I looked down over the steep cliff face onto the jungle below, and then beyond to the lush hillsides spread out like a green patchwork blanket. Crickets buzzed loudly in the canopy. Cattle and goats grazed in the clearings. Gaulins and John Crows dotted the sky overhead.

"You don't have to go call a duppy if you are afraid, you know!" Bredda Man said, looking closely at me to make sure that I was OK.

He made his concern sound so pathetic and absurd that we both started laughing till tears came to our eyes. When we finally settled down and I thought we were going forward, he looked at me again, with his left eyebrow raised in a pretend look of concern, and we both started laughing all over again. Bredda Man repeated this little joke over and over again, until he was sure I was relaxed and feeling totally safe with him.

When we finally stood up to go on, we both felt light and happy.

Bredda Man turned off the main track and went onto a narrow pathway partly hidden by the overhanging rocks. After a few more minutes, I saw the entrance to a large cave.

Bredda Man stopped at the entrance. He took some fresh green bissy (kola nuts) out of his bag and gave them to me to chew on while we gathered branches to build a fire.

The bitter juice of the kola nut is taken by warriors in West Africa before they march into battle. It induces a trance-like focus. It also tastes so bad that it induces vomiting. I had to really concentrate to keep myself from throwing up.

As soon as we had a good, strong fire going, Bredda Man sat down. He motioned for me to sit opposite him and then he told me to pay close attention.

"You must go down into the cave by yourself to call the duppy. The duppy you are going to look for is not a ghost. It is an angel being, and the task is to see it for yourself.

"There are many angelic forces inside of us that can connect us to a greater good in life, but until we meet these powers we can't take the help they offer us. They are like keys that we don't know what they are for or how to use them. And some of us are scared of these keys inside of us. So the symbol I show you will help you to find a powerful healing key.

"When I tell you to go on, go down through the cave till you find the place where it opens out wide and when you look up you can see the sky again. There will be a circle of bare ground in the clearing. Go and sit in the circle. Imagine this symbol I will show you and focus on it.

"After you are sitting beneath the stars and you keep imagining this symbol, draw the symbol in the earth. Then something will appear in the circle. It could be a light, a person, an animal, a bird—or anything. It will focus its movements and attention on you. It will try to frighten you, but stand up and look at it without fear, so you can know what it is. Study it carefully, and when you are sure that you know what you have seen, come back straight away."

I was chewing the bissy while Bredda Man explained everything and I noticed it was easy to absorb and remember what he said. I listened carefully to Bredda Man and understood clearly what I had to do.

He asked me to repeat back to him everything he had said, and when he was satisfied with what I told him, he carefully drew the symbol in the earth.

As I started to practice imagining the symbol, I felt the air around me grow crisp and clear like ice. My body felt light and strong. It tingled with nervous excitement. I managed to swallowed the last of the bitter pulp from the kola nuts. Then I felt ready to face the unknown.

Bredda Man stood at the entrance to the cave. He said he would watch over the symbol until I returned. He told me to go into the cave.

A smoothly trodden path at the back of the cave led straight and slightly downward into the mountain. I could walk upright for a while, but then the walls got closer and the darkness got colder. The light of the fire at the entrance quickly faded into the blackness. I was in total darkness.

I made my way through the tunnel, touching the damp, smooth walls every now and then for reassurance. It wasn't long before I entered a place where the tunnel seemed to get wider and higher. The air became softer and there was a slight breeze.

In another step I was out of the tunnel and in a small clearing. Sheer cliff walls towered above on all sides. I looked up and was surprised to see the stars shining brightly overhead and, by their light, the dim outline of a large open circle.

All at once, small points of light, like the stars, blinked open all around me. The darkness had come alive! I was surrounded by many watching eyes.

I stepped into the circle and sat down in the center. I drew the symbol on the bare ground in front of me and then closed my eyes and focused my thoughts inwardly on it.

As soon as I closed my eyes, I heard the rustling of something moving around in the walls of the cliffs. I lost my focus and opened my eyes. The circle was no longer as dark as before. Now I could make out its shape more clearly, and beyond it I could see that there were natural ledges, like shelves, in the cliff walls.

Suddenly, without any warning, I felt the damp, hot breath of a large animal on the back of my neck. I wheeled around. Nothing there!

"That did not feel at all like a duppy," I thought. I listened nervously. It was perfectly still.

I closed my eyes and tried to visualize the symbol several times. But each time my thoughts drifted off into fearful imaginings. I kept on trying to focus on the symbol until my body finally relaxed. Then the symbol seemed to take on a life of its own. When I opened my eyes, I could still see the symbol I had made inwardly for a few seconds.

High up in the cliff walls something stirred again. There was the sound of flapping, of great wings. A huge, dark shape swooped down out of the blackness. It landed with a soft thud directly in front of me. The creature took a few steps toward me and then stopped dead still. It was a John Crow!

I stood my ground. We stared at each other. I thought the bird might be sick because he didn't behave like a normal wild bird would act up close to a person. Then I smelled an intense odor—a powerful, sour, carrion stench that made me gag. I felt nausea begin to rise up into my throat.

Even though the cave was cool, sweat began to pour off me. I closed my eyes and tried to imagine the symbol again. But instead, I suddenly remembered my dream of a John Crow flying into the sun and becoming the light.

When I opened my eyes the John Crow was gone. Far away, moving around me along the outer edge of the circle I saw a small light. It looked like a peeny wolly (firefly). As it moved slowly closer, it got bigger until it was about the size of a football. It stayed the same height off the ground, hovering steadily and shedding a pale light around the whole area.

I started to get nervous because I wasn't sure whether I had found a duppy or not. I would certainly feel foolish if I returned to Bredda Man with a only peeny wolly story.

Something deep inside suddenly urged me to leave and energized me instantly into action.

I felt a bit disoriented, as if I had overslept and had forgotten it was a school day. I turned back the way I had come, walking through the tunnel as quickly as I could in the darkness.

The way back seemed shorter than the way in, and soon I saw the glow of the firelight at the cave mouth up ahead.

When I came out of the cave Bredda Man was sitting by the fire next to the symbol he had drawn in the earth. He told me to sit down and close my eyes.

I heard him start to sing softly and felt a strong tingling vibration on my skin.

"Open your eyes, John Crow." He said.

On the ground between us was a huge John Crow feather.

Bredda Man said I should take up the feather and dance with it. He told me to imagine I was a John Crow and I was flying. He told me to copy the movements of the bird I had seen as if it was inside me.

I held the feather and I danced.

Looking at the feather as I danced, I remembered the movements of the duppy John Crow. I also remembered the sickening smell.

Then Bredda Man showed me how to use the feather to cleanse my body whenever I felt sick or afraid. He told me the duppy John Crow chose me because he wanted me to keep dancing for his people. My dancing would ensure the survival of the John Crows.

I closed my eyes and danced for the John Crow. I danced and danced, for what seemed like a long time. And then I opened my eyes. I looked around. It was dark and … I was shocked to find … I was still in the circle! I thought I must have been dreaming and I wondered how long I had been there.

Something deep inside suddenly urged me to leave and energized me instantly into action.

I turned back the way I had come, walking through the tunnel as quickly as I could in the darkness, thinking how strange it was that I had been dreaming everything.

The way back seemed shorter than the way in, and soon I saw the glow of the firelight at the cave mouth up ahead.

When I came out of the cave Bredda Man was sitting by the fire next to the symbol he had drawn in the earth.

I told him everything. He half-smiled and watched me intently, nodding his head seriously as he listened.

Then he gave me some eetee otee apple and water. I had to force myself to eat it because my nose still remembered the stink of the John Crow. When I finished the last bite of the apple, I was feeling really anxious about what would happen next.

Bredda Man told me to sit down and close my eyes. When he started to sing softly, I felt a strong tingling vibration on my skin.

"Open your eyes, John Crow," he said.

Bredda Man was staring intensely at the symbol he had drawn in the ground. A huge John Crow feather—just like the one in the dream—lay next to the symbol. He gave me the feather and told me to dance with it as I had done in the dream.

I danced until I felt as if I was about to drift away. I felt I was high up in the air with a lot of space all around me. I started to sweat profusely.

Bredda Man told me to come back and sit down. He began rubbing his hands over my face, really hard, so that my skin was pressed hard against my skull. He said he was rubbing some medicine into me. He rubbed my back, arms and legs until I felt totally present and strong—like I did before I had gone into the cave and drifted into another world.

We drank some more water together. Then we put out the fire and walked home in silence.

As we came to the last ridge of the hills that led down from the mountains, Bredda Man turned and spoke in a serious voice as he strongly massaged my neck, shoulders, arms and back again.

"That feather is a powerful gift, little bredda. Every day… Dance … Dance with your feather, John Crow. As you dance, you will feel the John Crow grow stronger. When you feel the charge of energy in your body, you sit down and meditate."

Then Bredda Man asked me to tell him everything I had learned from going into the cave and calling the duppy. When he was satisfied with what I told him, he continued to tell me about the meaning of the feather gift and how the John Crow dance prepared my body and focused my energy to heal.

"The first gift given to you by Creation was the lizard's gift. You completed that gift by accepting it. That was like the river flowing down the mountain and watering the valley. Now the water can produce fruits and vegetables and that requires harvesting so they can be used for food.

"It is like when we seek for the keys to direction in life, this natural flow and growth is the first gift from the Creator to us. Then when we consciously search, we find the keys to complete the work Creation started.

"For the first key, the gift of the lizard, you did not need to be conscious. But to reap the harvest, to respect and honor that gift, you have to consciously find the next key. That is what we are doing here.

"Now you will see the John Crow around you grow stronger, too. That is our job as awake human beings. ... When we dance for the animal beings ... they stay strong and they can help us to fight off our diseases and all kind of bad mindedness. Dance with your John Crow feather around the Elders' Fire. Dance so your brethren know the Elders' Fire. This way your spiritual expression is healing all Creation. Out of this dance of yours will come true meditation.

"It is the same when we hunt. We are searching for living food. This food is given to us by the Creator as a gift, it is a living connection to a living God. When we eat the flesh of this gift, we have a sacred responsibility to all the family of this creature to complete the gift that will keep them strong.

"If we dance for an animal then we establish a foundation through that animal we can draw on and also help other people. Then we have a living foundation for wisdom. It takes time to get accustomed to an animal in this way, so don't talk about what is going on till after you get to know the John Crow very well."

Bredda Man watched my expression to see how I was feeling. I was feeling very tired but, strangely, I also felt awake and alive.

"You must try to find out everything you can about your John Crow from now on and remember it! How long do you believe it is going to take to get accustomed to the John Crow?"

I was confident about the work that lay ahead. "Six months" jumped out of my mouth before I knew I had said it.

"Every day... and at least ten minutes each time," he added.

Bredda Man told me he was going away into the mountains and would be back when I finished my assignment.

"Then," he said, "there will be even more important healing work for us to do."

# 14

# John Crow Speaks

IT SEEMED THAT my work was just beginning. By using the symbol to call the duppy I had entered the realm of the unconscious and I had returned safely with the form I needed to develop my own insight and power.

My new insights changed the way I experienced the world. I felt a sense of vast expansion. But I felt disconnected from everything in my ordinary life. The sense of disorientation that stalked the borders of my experience like a watchful guardian challenged me to bring my experiences back into my familiar world in some useful way.

Although I knew that fear of my own thoughts and dramas would never again hold hostage my purpose in life, simply going back to my ordinary life could not relieve the isolation I felt.

Every day I danced and spoke for Creation. I meditated. I drew and I wrote. During that time I also roamed the hills of Jamaica studying the habits of the John Crows. I read as much as I could about the John Crows and found references about him as a symbol in the mythologies and traditions of many ancient cultures. The more I persevered with my work, the more I felt the connection to the John Crow become a living foundation for my understanding. I began to see that creating a living foundation for knowledge was a way my insights could become useful.

Bredda Man called the insights hidden in our habits and impulses the "seeds of wisdom." These ancient seeds had been planted at birth, but they would never grow under a care driven by greed or fear. Only a conscious will with a sincere and dedicated heart could bring these precious fruits into the world. And so with an opened heart, I started to speak for the John Crow.

*  *  *

### Speaking for the John Crow

Our clan soars highest among the birds.

We do not struggle to create something new as others do. We celebrate old age and death where others fear and postpone it, always feverishly trying to prolong life.

Our task is to observe the predator within. We hunt for the inevitable uncertainty, waiting for the second of carelessness that will betray weakness and call in the predators. With great patience we examine what chooses to force change within our hearts.

The discipline of a clear heart feeds on the death of insensitivity, laziness and despair to keep the dead from infecting the living. We keep the hurts of the past from contaminating the fragile newborn present. We nourish ourselves with understanding, digesting the skeletons left to wither in our being by the sins of our fathers.

All creatures that live upon the earth must hurt others when they hunt or gather food. We soar all day in the clouds and harm no living creature.

Others, seeing our patient circling as fruitless introspection, choose wild action and the thrill of the hunt. With eternity stretching out before us like a chasm, we choose instead to fill our moments with the pleasures of true understanding, patiently cleansing our heart of decay and disease.

Ferocious introspection, honesty and self scrutiny are required to keep us alive in this task. Each time we find an attitude that threatens our inner environment with its deathly stench, we accept and digest it in a spirit of patient contemplation and peace. The lonely rigors and discipline of seeking death within ourselves has made us a homeless clan.

A great yearning draws us to the secret hurts and pains of those who cannot bear the constant taste of death in their mouth. We know death as a friend. If we can be compassionate to death itself, who can we not love?

Our path is the end of seeking and achieving. We serve all creatures without preference for status or power. We lift up the crass, the callous, the sluggish and take them on wings to touch the Sun.

We spend our days in the subtle realms of contemplation that inspire changes from within. Each new inspiration heralds the death of an unwholesome habit or intellectual attitude that has stunk up the living wilderness of the heart's innocence. Then, this fragile world of life and innocence can be renewed each day to health and cleanliness.

We celebrate life by digesting what is cast aside, what has lost its luster, beauty, strength, hope—love gone cold, youth faded, the hero without motivation, unfulfilled dreams. All that is wasted is food for us. We use what has turned away from life to feed purpose in ourselves.

All this talk about death is not some morbid fascination. There is great joy in the lessons and celebration of death, my brother. Who else uses as nourishment each static or unhealthy feeling, each negative attitude or thought, each dead thing within themselves or society by digesting it, cleansing it away, breaking it down and understanding it, so that it can benefit and educate others? The familiar world is healed each time we devour, digest, and understand a deadly attitude that has held someone's life at bay.

We are the healers within every family, who show how the pain, shame and ridicule of generations can be digested and overcome so that new life can take hold. This is our gift to the world.

There is no reason to ever fear death! It is the greatest teacher of change, the most nourishing of ideas, and truly food for the soul. There is great joy in the lessons and celebration of death, my brother!

But few will seek death's company as a teacher. Fewer still can use death as nourishment.

And only you will fear no one, John Crow, because no one can defeat death.

\* \* \*

During the times when Bredda Man had been away, I looked back on what I had learned and always saw the value of what we did. Then I would look forward, with both fear and excitement, to our next meeting. This time, something inside me had changed. I was no longer anxious or excited about our next meeting. Now I had a hunger inside that could only be fed by the insight and understanding I gained through my own conscious efforts and study. I was no longer working to impress Bredda Man, or anyone else. I was no longer working to prove anything. There was a certainty now for walking the path of my own making.

As I sat alone meditating, I realized that this was part of Bredda Man's teaching, like going into the forest to listen to nature or going into the circle to call a duppy. Now I was using the tools he had given me to develop my own potential for understanding, creativity, and insight.

This work of building and using the tools I was given, was what Bredda Man called Leaving Egypt and the Journey through the Wilderness to the Promised Land. It is the journey that everyone makes to create a living knowledge—the blessings of the wilderness.

Suddenly I knew where Bredda man had been leading me all along. He had been leading me toward the greatest gift of all of his teachings—my independence.

In the bush, no other person stands between the Living God and the wilderness of our hearts. There, in the free living wilderness, without the protection of human devices, we can know god's mercy and blessing.

When we have established a living knowledge rooted in our experience of the wilderness, we bless ourself in the land. That is why it is said by the living God, "Whoever blesses himself in the land, Shall bless himself by the True God."

I knew in my bones that my work with Bredda Man would continue soon enough. I knew we would walk together when he returned from the mountains. And I knew without a doubt that when we met again, we would meet in the Promised Land.

what was happening in this space as we walked together. I felt Bredda Man knew my thoughts and feelings. Every gesture of his body echoed my awareness and returned to me as some deeply familiar aspect of our relationship together.

I remembered the plumb line and noticed our walking and our breathing both had the same elements—Formlessness/balance and a polarity between left and right, in and out. I began to allow my breathing to be part of our walking.

I was surprised to find that we had arrived at the road that led up the hill to my house. I looked around. Bredda Man was smiling at me. It was a radiant smile, charged by a lightning bolt of energy.

"Eat something when you reach home!" he reminded me, and then he walked off.

I ran up the hill without any effort at all. When I reached the top, I suddenly realized I had sprinted up the entire hill and I wasn't even out of breath. Everything looked vibrant. There was no happy or sad in this knowing, no good or bad. Everything simply was being itself. I remember seeing the entire mountain and all its living forms as part of one great, alive space and time. I heard from a still point deep inside me: "Holy Land."

I remembered what Bredda Man said about eating something and headed for the kitchen. I found some fish fritters left over from last night's dinner. I was not hungry, but I took one, and as I started to chew, my appetite slowly returned. The keen awareness I had felt subsided back into my body, like a light that, having emerged from the center of my being to awaken my body, was now returning to the darkness deep within me again.

On that day I remember feeling that I had for the first time started to take responsibility for the development of "substance" within myself. I realized, too, that Bredda Man had used his own substance to show me how the mood swings and attitudes of positive and negative could be controlled. He had shown me a focus that was based on Formlessness.

I felt the immensity of what Bredda Man had shared with me. The knowing I felt was without precedent in my life experience. I had learned to value what I feel and to recognize it as the source of my own well-being. I had learned to listen to my Heart.

# 9

# The Gift of Understanding

BREDDA MAN HAD PROMISED to show me how to set up calabans and springes in the forest. These are traps made with
wood and twine that were used to catch doves and partridges.
I was looking forward to seeing him again, and when the
weekend came I raced all the way down the hill to his cabin.

When I found Bredda Man he was carving. He had already
made several small pieces. A scraggly-looking lump of half-
formed wood caught my eye. I asked him what it was. He said
it came from a John Crow and only the John Crow could tell
me what it was.

I was about to ask him more about the strange piece of
wood when there was shouting outside and some boys, all
about my age, came running up to the house. Following them,
their mothers appeared with groceries—coffee, nutmeg, con-
densed milk and some soursop—for Bredda Man.

After the ladies said their howdy-dos they came inside to
brew some coffee and make soursop juice. Then there was a
lot of talking and sipping and tasting and talking among
themselves—just to make sure everything was really good
before they gave it to Bredda Man. While this was going on
inside among the ladies, the rest of us retreated outside.
Bredda Man took up his carving and started to tell us a story
as he continued to work.

## The Girl and the Ugly Fruit

A beautiful young girl named Tamah lives in the forest. She knows all the ways of the forest and she knows the names of all the creatures in the forest. They all love her and she is happy. One day an old man named Dagah comes into the forest. He brings a gift for her. It is a fruit. But it looks ugly and it smells bad. Tamah can't eat it, so she buries it in the ground behind her house.

Soon a big tree is growing there where Tamah buried the ugly fruit. It bears plenty ugly fruit. Nobody will eat the fruit. The seeds like their new home. They grow and grow, and soon the forest fills up of the big trees. Tamah gets frightened because the forest starts to look ugly and smell bad, too. Her heart is breaking and she runs away to tell herself, it's her fault everything is ugly.

She runs deep into the forest where nobody ever goes. There she meets up with an old mongoose. His name is Maas Chasan and he is guardian of a sacred cave. After Maas Chasan listens to Tamah's story, he feels sorry for her. Tamah asks Maas Chasan what she must do. Maas Chasan says, "Listen, Miss Tammy, I can't give you answers. Everyone who comes to me must find the answers for themselves. But if you are willing to work hard, I know where to send you to find the answers."

Tamah feels glad even if Maas Chasan couldn't tell her the answers.

Maas Chasan tells Tamah to follow him and he takes her to visit Maas River. They follow Maas River through the forest from the lake high up into the mountains, down the waterfall, and through the bush all the way to the sea. Tamah is tired and she asks Maas Chasan why they follow the river so far. Maas Chasan asks her, "Which part of the river seems the most powerful to you?"